Wildcrafts

Wildcrafts

Leslie Linsley

Photographs by Jon Aron

Doubleday & Company, Inc., Garden City, New York 1977

Library of Congress Cataloging in Publication Data

Linsley, Leslie.
    Wildcrafts.
    1. Handicraft.   2. Nature craft.   I. Title.
TT157.L485   745.5   76-50777
ISBN: 0-385-12687-5
Library of Congress Number 76-50777

Book design by Jon Aron

Acknowledgment

While nature crafting is quite familiar, it is the personal approach of the individual crafters that makes each project unique. When working on this book I was fortunate to meet some wonderful fellow craftworkers who were happy to share their crafting experiences. It is this sharing that has made nature crafting more exciting, romantic, and fun, than it has ever been. Jon and I want to thank Ethel Margolies, Ann Jones, Henry Petzel, Beth Trudeau, Craig Kay, Danielle Frommer, Michael Butler, Mara Cary, Rachael Love Mitchell, Sally Pfeifer, Jane Kasten, Charles McGuire, Elen Schwartz, Carl Moreus and Kathy-Kelm Cronin. Thanks also to Suzie, Dan Bills, Ruth Stick, The Brookfield Craft Center, and my editor, Karen Van Westering.

L.L.

Contents

Basket by Mara Cary

Wildcrafts

Introduction

It's early fall in New England and I am distracted from my work. From my desk against the windows I can see the leaves turning colors of wine and golden yellow and burning orange, and it is unbelievably beautiful. Some of the maple trees have already lost their leaves and there are acorns scattered everywhere. Three squirrels are taking full advantage of this bounty, and a familiar chipmunk scurries under the front steps. Only a few birds remain. It is quiet compared to the full orchestra that celebrated the arrival of spring. It is an impressive sight that living here in Connecticut, I have seen over and over again all my life.

But you don't have to live in the country to appreciate nature's gifts. The flowers that grow in vast country fields are often found in more common areas. A roadside, schoolyards, your back yard, a vacant lot, even cracks in the sidewalk can yield a sampling of the same wildflowers. Look again wherever you are. You may see something that you *knew* wasn't there before. When out driving take along clippers and a plastic bag. Perhaps even, work gloves and hiking shoes will come in handy.

I have always been a curious observer of nature. I've spent pleasant days as a flower gatherer not knowing their botanical names, but appreciating the harmony of nature. I have taken great delight in discovering a familar face, and have enjoyed the occasional challenge of trying to identify one that I did not recognize. Sometimes hearing the names of the flowers and herbs is enough to make you want to become involved. How can anyone ignore such great sounding names; bayberry, buttercup, sage, lemon verbina, cinnamon, lavender? I love the word "wildcrafting". It is a term used for gathering and blending herbs and extracts for medicinal purposes. Some of the crafters who work with nature refer to their material in their own way. Rachael Mitchell calls them the "wildies". My preference is "wildcrafts".

You can go for a walk and pick a bouquet of flowers. You can gather pine cones in the woods. And practically no one comes home from the seashore without some shells. The bouquet eventually wilts and dies and is discarded. Its pleasure-giving time is extended a week or so beyond the first joy of discovery. The pine cones may be set in a basket and the shells in a jar. Occasionally they are reminders of a pleasant day. But their potential goes far beyond. Craft projects made from natural materials are not new. But they are endless.

I think that most of us refer to crafting with natural materials as using bits of nature such as leaves, pine cones, flowers, shells, in their natural state and incorporating them into decorative or useful objects.

Unlike many other crafts, crafting with natural materials does not require any special training. Almost everyone, at one time or another, has made something from nature. Some of these projects have been quite simple, often traditional in design and requiring little time to produce satisfactory results. Many people have a great deal of knowledge about how to work with the materials and have created quite unusual items. And then there are talented artists and designers who have applied their creativity to this area of crafting, producing unusual designs for ordinary objects.

There is almost no project that has not been done many times before. After all, the natural materials have always been there for people to use. Many of the handcrafted objects that we make for decoration or accessory were made in colonial times for everyday use. Simple baskets were made to carry specific objects, and the designs and methods that we use today are no different from those used by the Indians. Gourds were dried and scooped out for use as bottles and cooking utensils long before pottery came into being.

The process involved in making a crafted piece often has more value than the item itself. Take for example the bayberry candle. From a commercial point of view, there is no justification for the time it takes to produce one small candle. True, it will burn longer and brighter than any you can buy in a store, but we are used to evaluating our time in terms of money. Can we afford to take a day to gather enough berries for cooking and extracting wax for just a few candles? The question is not can we afford the time. Those who have taken the time would probably say, "Can we afford not to?"

There is something quite special about having lemon verbena tea with a friend, knowing that the herb was grown in her garden and that the cups were made from the earth's clay. Someone lovingly planted the herbs, tended them on a sunny, summer day, maybe had some good day dreams along the way. Another crafter spent time digging clay from the beach, brought it home and shaped and turned it into cups.

The craft projects that follow are the results of sharing. The people involved in the natural crafting experience have shared their personal techniques and offered guidance through helpful instructions and individual design ideas. These projects represent a sampling of nature crafts using materials from different areas. The intention is to expand the design possibilities for projects using materials familiar to everyone. I hope you will grow through the crafting process and continue with some new ideas of your own.

On the Woodland Floor

No matter what time of year, a walk in the woods will always yield a variety of natural materials for craft projects. A pine grove in particular can be an interesting place to visit if you are lucky enough to live near one. It is usually quiet and peaceful, and the smell of the pine needles that provide a luxurious carpet underfoot adds to the atmosphere.

Take along a plastic bag for collecting material. Look carefully. There are all kinds of interesting fungi. Even if you don't know exactly what projects you will make, collect a variety of things that interest you. You might see pieces of bark that could be used with a woven hanging. Interesting dried pieces of wood are always useful, sometimes in a small terrarium or in a wood assemblage. I have collected bags full of feathers that have fallen from the trees. Sometimes they are the same color as the earth and can be quite camouflaged. The natural color of many materials keep them from being obvious if you aren't looking for anything specific. There is of course a wide variety of leaves in wooded areas, depending on the different trees and the area you live in. Gather as many different kinds as you can find. Acorns, nuts, berries, twigs and branches, the bark of a fallen birch tree, are all potential craft material. Pieces of moss, lichen, fungi, and mushrooms can also be used. When picking the mushrooms, lift them carefully in order to preserve them. If you are not gentle the top will fall off. If this happens, save it. The top of the mushroom is all that will be used to make spore prints. Look for tiny mushrooms that might be growing in a cluster. These can be used in a miniature diorama or simply dried and put on display. Remember, many mushrooms found in the woods are not edible. Unless you are knowledgeable in the field, don't take a chance on eating them.

Different pine trees have distinctly different kinds of cones. Collect them in varying sizes. The ones you find will be determined by what is available in your area. The balsam needles are especially fragrant, and you might like to fill a bag for sachet making.

Ferns can also be found in wooded areas. They are beautifully delicate, can be pressed and dried successfully, and are worth collecting.

Materials needed:
3" wooden trinket cylindrical box
½- or ¼-inch paint brush
White acrylic paint
Small piece of fine sandpaper
Spray varnish
Large mushroom cap

There are hundreds of varieties of mushrooms that are commonly found in the woods primarily during the months of August and September. Mushrooms do not have seeds but reproduce by spores that are released from the underside of the "umbrella". When placed on a surface such as wood or paper the released spores create a pattern resembling the underside of the mushroom. If the mushroom has a brown underside, the released spores will usually create a brown design. If the under-

Mushroom releasing spores onto a trinket box.

side is white or cream color, the design will usually be that color. Therefore, you might use a dark brown paint rather than white if your mushroom is light in color.

Begin by sanding the box so that it is smooth to the touch. Wipe off the dust from sanding, then give the box a coat of white (or a dark color) paint. Acrylic paint is a water-base paint that comes in a tube or a jar and flows on evenly while covering in one coat. Paint the bottom and top of the box separately and let dry thoroughly, usually about twenty minutes. Rinse your brush in warm water. When the outside is dry you might like to paint the inside in a contrasting color.

When the box is dry sand it very lightly so that it will again be smooth. Often dust and paint particles dry on the surface of the paint causing imperfections in the finish. A light sanding with the fine sandpaper will be sufficient. If you feel that the box needs another coat of paint, apply the second coat the same way and let it dry thoroughly before sanding again. Blow away any sand dust so that the top of the box is clean.

Carefully lift the top of the mushroom away from the stem. Try not to break it as it is quite delicate. Center the mushroom over the top of the box and then carefully put it down directly on the box top. Once it is placed in position, it cannot be removed and placed down again. The spores will begin to release the second it makes contact with the surface and by moving it you will disturb the design that you are creating.

Place a large water glass over the box so that the spores will not blow away if there is a wind or air circulation in the room. This will also insure a clear, strong design. Leave it alone overnight. Then remove the glass and carefully pick up the mushroom. The top of your box should have a spore design as if painted on the box. If the design is not exactly the way you would like it to be, it can be wiped away and replaced with another mushroom. Once you have a good print do not touch it.

Hold the top of the box about two feet away from you and spray it with clear spray varnish. This can be a matte or glossy finish, depending on your taste. The coating of varnish will preserve the design permanently. Once dry, you can apply two or three more coats of varnish to further protect it. You might like to finish off the box with a little decoupage. Simply cut out some mushroom prints from a book, print, or greeting card and glue them around the outside of the box. Use the same spray varnish to cover the decoupage designs. You will need five or six coats of varnish for this. After each coat is completely dry sand over the surface very lightly. Use the same fine sandpaper and be sure to sand gently so that you will not sand away the paper designs.

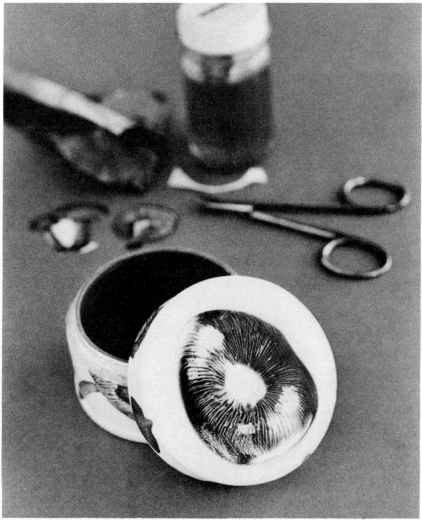

Design made from mushroom spores.

Spore Prints

Ethel Margolies knows her mushrooms.

"I love mushrooms. Oh, they are so delicious, but I haven't eaten any for years. When I was very young I used to gather and eat mushrooms. I knew which were the edible ones and which were poisonous. But I was fooled. I ate some very bad mushrooms and they made me very sick", Ethel Margolies explained all this while showing me the results of her main involvement with mushrooms today; her beautiful mushroom spore prints. It was a visual treat visiting with Mrs. Margolies in her old Connecticut home filled with plants, unusual artifacts, and paintings. Ethel P. Margolies is an artist of varied talents. Her oils are hung in one part of the house, but her collages dominate. And if one looks carefully, mushroom spore prints can be found in several of the collages. "I'm always ripping paper. First I make the mushroom prints then I usually rip off a few to include in the collages. Aren't mushrooms great?" she said. We walked out to the back of her yard and sure enough she emerged holding two newly sprouted finds. "These are very

When making spore prints keep the mushroom covered.

young. If I had left them alone they would have become quite large." We went back into the house to make some prints. Ethel said that a friend had called to ask for detailed instructions for making the prints. "It's so silly. There's nothing to it. The mushrooms do all the work," she told me as she placed the mushrooms, with stems removed, side by side on a piece of heavy matte board. Next a large glass cake cover was placed over the mushrooms so that the air would not cause a swirling effect which can be seen on some of the prints. When left uncovered the motion of air causes the spores to move away from the area directly under the mushroom. This will create a smoky effect that can also be quite nice. The glass cover that was used for this is a lovely handblown one that Ethel treasures. It is so beautiful to see the sun shining on the glass, creating shadows around the mushrooms as they release their spores.

Before placing the mushrooms on the paper decide how you would like to see the design. You may like one that is created by

Mushroom spore print by Ethel P. Margolies.

placing several mushrooms close together, or you may prefer
the beauty of a single mushroom print.

Ethel spread before us the different spore prints that she had
made. It is amazing how many different shapes, sizes and variety of designs you can experiment with. She used various colored background papers for the different mushroom colors.
Some prints were discarded as experiments, others had been
matted and were ready for framing and hanging. Any paper
can be used, but for framing, heavier paper, like illustration
board, works best.

While they are all sprayed after the print is made, it seems
that they are still quite delicate. If not handled properly, they
will smudge and the definition of the gills will be spoiled. Several clear Krylon spray coatings, matte varnish, or hair spray
will protect the prints so they will last permanently.

Before leaving, Ethel gave me a greeting card that she had
had printed. The background color is red and there is a single
white mushroom spore print in the center. *(Color plate #1.)* A
friend drove her to the printers while she held the print in tact
so that it would not smudge before it could be photographed.

Drying Mushrooms

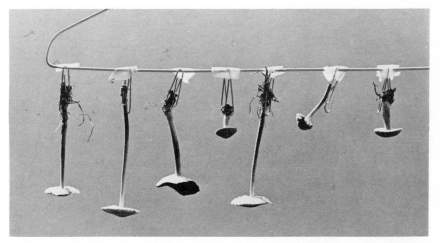

I experimented with different ways to dry mushrooms and can only pass along my findings. If you have done it in a better way, please continue to do so. I happen to think that mushrooms are adorable. I discovered that when dried they are even more delightful. They shrivel up a bit and have a comical appearance. Mushrooms have been known as far back as there is any written word, and for centuries have been used for cooking in almost every country in the world.

Mushrooms grow in cool, moist areas, usually away from direct light. After a rainy period it is easy to find mushrooms of almost every size and shape. The smaller sizes are best for this project. Many types of wild mushrooms are edible, but others are deadly poison. If you are not familiar with the harmless kinds, save all your mushroom hordes for crafting.

If you pick your mushrooms on a dry, sunny day, air drying works best. Using a regular wire clothes hanger clip or tape the mushroom stems to the hanger. Masking tape holds them well, or you can use paper clips to hold them to the wire. Keep a bit of space between them so that the air can circulate. Then simply hang them on a tree branch or other convenient spot in the sun. Leave them there for an hour or so until they feel dry to the touch. They will begin to lose their moisture and become tough. It does not take long for mushrooms to dry out. After they are dry but still hanging, spray them lightly on all sides with a clear varnish spray. This will keep them from shriveling up com-

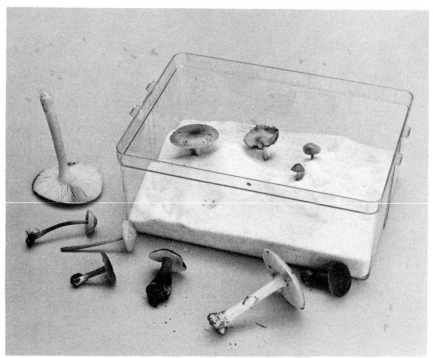

Mushrooms dry in minutes when placed in silica gel.

pletely as well as prevent the moisture in the air from being reabsorbed. Once the mushrooms are dry if they are not treated and there is moisture in the air they may begin to spoil within several hours. If the spray is a glossy varnish, it will give the mushrooms a shiny coating. If you prefer to keep their more natural look use a matte spray varnish.

Another way to dry mushrooms is to place them in silica gel. This is a drying agent that is available in craft stores. Using a plastic box, pour a thin layer of the silica gel on the bottom of the box. Place each mushroom into the box head first. Slowly pour the silica gel around the mushrooms so that it begins to cover the caps. Fill the box so that the stems are covered. Put a top on the box or cover it with an air-tight material such as plastic film. Leave this for about a half hour. The mushrooms will dry out very quickly. Check by pulling one out carefully and touching it. If it is not dry enough, put it back into the silica gel and wait a while longer. When the mushrooms are dry take them out of the box and blow the silica gel off of them. This fine powdery material has a tendency to cling to the mushrooms but can be removed by brushing lightly. Spray these mushrooms with the varnish spray. If you do not spray them immediately, the moisture in the air will be absorbed back into them and they will become soggy and rotten. Once sprayed, the mushrooms can be set aside in a plastic bag until you are ready to use them if you are not planning to do a project right away.

Woodland Diorama

*Dried bark, moss, mushrooms, and pine will
be used to create a diorama in a photo cube.*

Once you have dried some small mushrooms you might like to
use them in a miniature woodland scene. When walking in the
woods stop for a moment and look down. Look at the tiny patch
by your feet. You might see a twig, some acorns, a few mushrooms, a leaf, fungi and old pieces of fallen bark. It is this random quality that is typical of the woodland floor. You can re-
create this character in a miniature scene. The materials have
dried up and fallen to the ground. Collect small objects that you
can use. Be sure to gather a variety so that you'll have enough to
choose from when arranging them.

A small plastic photo cube is perfect to use as a display case
for a woodland scene. Sphagnum moss is excellent as a filler because it will hold the dried material. This is a green spongy substance and can be purchased in hobby or craft stores. You might
like to use peat moss or potting soil as well.

Begin by covering the bottom of the cube with an inch of dirt. Place the sphagnum moss here and there on top of the dirt. Put the dried material into the cube so that it looks right. That same random quality found in the woods should exist in your diorama. The mushrooms should look as though they have just sprung up. A leaf might be dropped into place as though it had just fallen to the ground. A twig, a piece of dried bark can balance the scene. Do not use large objects that might overpower the others. For a dramatic effect, place the finished project on a table and light it from behind.

Fungi Art

Ann Jones is an artist But painting pictures is only a small part of what Ann does. And everything she turns her creative energy to is done extremely well. There is a degree of professionalism rarely found in such diversity of interests. All around her studio and home there is definite confirmation that Ann Jones lives here. She is tiny, but she comes across loud and clear. Bursting with enthusiasm as she talks about the activities she has been involved with, it is hard to believe that all the craft projects we see have been done by one person.

Ann's real love and involvement is with mushrooms. Upon walking into her home you are immediately aware that mushrooms are afoot. The shelves in the kitchen hold dried mushrooms, stone mushrooms, ceramic mushrooms. A mushroom collage on one wall catches your eye, then another, and still another. Step carefully, mushroom books lie open on the floor. A file box of spore prints is in use on the dining room table. Never have mushrooms looked more beautiful, nor have I ever been more aware of them. Can there really be so many different shapes, colors, sizes, textures? It is infectious. "There are many of us." Ann grins. "In fact there's a whole society of mushroom fanciers." Ann and her husband study mushrooms, eat mushrooms, give lectures on mushrooms, go on field trips stalking, collecting, cataloging, and examining mushrooms.

Sticking to the subject of crafting is difficult for me. It is so tempting to be diverted. But mushrooms are a main crafting subject in Ann's work, so it is not hard to come back to the subject at hand. In response to a question she jumps up, pulls out a small book from the bookshelf, and shows me the difference between lichen and poly pores. She imparts the knowledge with such ease that you know this is her territory. Before you can digest it all she's off to the studio. "I have something else to show you." Following her down the stairs she suddenly disappears into another room. In a small laundry room she opens boxes of collected poly pores. More mushrooms are drying. There is a mirrored shadow box in progress. It holds a few clusters of dried mushrooms.

Assemblage

The mushroom assemblages are quite exquisite. Ann says she spends a lot of time at junkyards and dumps looking for unusual pieces of wood or boxes to display the fungi. The one we have shown here is a type drawer; however you might want to make your own display case. Or you can adapt an interesting drawer by making small dividers that can be inserted into it. Paint the entire case either white or dark brown for a background setting.

Ann has a good sense of design when selecting and arranging the pieces of dried material. Look for things that interest you and arrange them in a pleasing way according to shape, size, and color. Glue them in place with any regular household glue such as Elmer's. Although they look unusual and exotic, a variety of fungi are not necessarily difficult to find. If you look carefully, you will find that most woods yield a variety of interesting material.

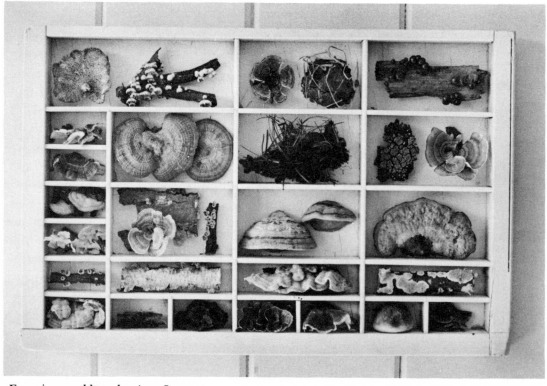

Fungi assemblage by Ann Jones.

"Now these are fun," Ann says back in the studio. "This is called artist's fungi." Those big oddly shaped growths that are often found attached to the base of a tree trunk are also known as Foamies Applanatus. They look like something right out of *Alice In Wonderland* and are found in all sizes and shapes. The picture is made on the underside and will be permanent once the fungi is dry and hard. Ann's are appropriately designed with mushroom scenes.

When I asked Ann what kind of tool she used to draw on the fungus she said, "Oh, it depends on where I am when I find it. Any sharp instrument, even a needle will work." When you go out looking for your fungi take along a drawing implement because the best time to do the art work is immediately upon finding the fungus while it is fresh and moist.

Lift the fungus gently from the tree trunk. It should come off easily. Don't touch the underside as you will leave a fingerprint. The surface is easily bruised. Decide on the design or picture that you would like to make. There is no need to feel intimidated if you are not an artist. The nature of the material should encourage you to create even the simplest design. Make your

Get the message? Fungi art by Ann Jones.

Art on fungi by Ann Jones.

design on the fungus by gently scribing, thus bruising, the surface. You don't have to bear down as the fungus is delicate. What you are doing is bruising, not drawing, in order to create the design. The bruise marks will be darker having penetrated the surface, which will remain light.

Place the fungus on a table in a warm, dry area. A furnace room is perfect. As it dries—usually in a couple of days, depending on size—the fungus will harden and your drawing will be permanent. The fungus will lighten a bit as it dries, but the contrast of the dark bruises against a lighter background will remain.

Isn't that great? That's all there is to it. I'll bet you can't wait to get to a wooded area to find your fungi.

Ann disappears again, returning with a package. "I don't do this anymore so I'll give you one of my crafting secrets." Somehow you know that she'd tell you even if she were doing it still. She is more than happy to share her discoveries.

She unwraps a package of framed slate gravestone rubbings. "Can you guess how they're done?" They are indeed rubbings on slate, but how did she do it? She can't wait to tell. Smiling again she holds up a piece of black tissue paper with a rubbing identical to the one on the slate. "I love it," she says. "It's so simple." Maybe simple, but very clever.

Gravestone rubbing on slate by Ann Jones.

To do this project, you will need a piece of wax or a wax crayon sold in art supply stores for gravestone rubbing, a piece of black tissue paper, a piece of slate large enough for a design, and framing material if you want to frame it. If not, the slate can be hung as is.

Old gravestones are especially good for this project. The designs are usually interesting and visiting an old graveyard can be fun. If you will be passing through an old town, take along your crayon and tissue and check out cemeteries. Recommended time: Daytime.

Place a piece of black tissue paper on the gravestone and rub over it. The impression will be white or gray. Next spread

Gravestone rubbing on tissue before transferring to slate.

Elmer's glue on the slate. Lay the tracing impression side up on the glue. Press it down and smooth the edges onto the slate so that you can't see them. Never, never, without being told, could anyone tell that the rubbing was not done directly on the slate. Once dry, the tissue rubbing will blend in with the slate's surface. You can hang the slate as is, or you can mount and frame it as Ann did.

Slate is available from roofing companies and sometimes at dumpyards. Odd shapes and pieces are the most interesting, and you might get leftovers for nothing. If you live in the northern part of New England, you might be able to find scraps at a nearby quarry.

Slate Relief

"When I was teaching crafts, my students really enjoyed making these." Ann picks up two slate relief pictures. "They're real easy to do and a lot of fun." All of Ann Jones' crafting techniques seem to have this wonderful combination of qualities. The results of her design ability, however, are what attracts us to the projects.

The slate pieces for this project are small scraps of interesting shapes and sizes. The shape of the slate often seems to inspire a design idea. Begin by drawing or tracing a design on the slate surface. After tracing a design from a book or similar source, rub chalk over the back of the paper. Lay this on the slate and go over your tracing with a pencil. The chalk outline will come off on the slate so that you will be able to see it. Since slate is really more gray in color than black, you might want to first blacken the surface with paint or India ink.

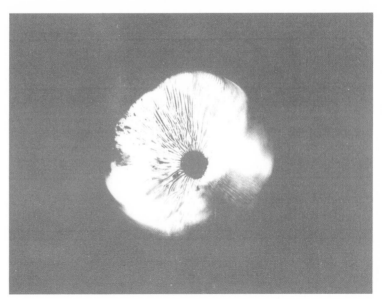

1. Spore print greeting card by Ethel Margolies

2. Spore print and decoupage trinket box

3. *Mushroom assemblage by Ann Jones*

4. *Pine sachets*

5. *Pressed leaf file box*

6. *Springtime gathering*

7. *Decorator tiles*

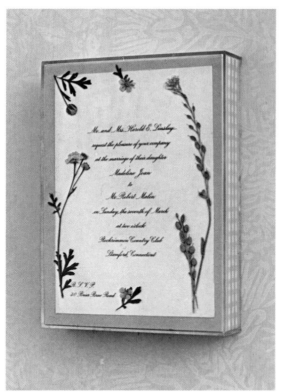

8. Wedding announcement

9. Wild cards

10. *Pressed flower collage*

11. *Leaded glass box by Craig Kay*

12. Pressed flower candles

13. Flower tray

14. Flower tray

15. Flower tray

To raise the design, you will gouge away the areas around the outside of the design. Using a wood-carving tool or other sharp implement, gouge away at the slate. It is quite soft and will not be difficult to remove. The design can be raised as much as you want. The more of the surrounding slate that you remove, the more your picture will be raised.

Ann's handcrafts have sold all over the country, but she is putting craft work aside in order to concentrate on her painting. I suspect, however, that she will always have a craft idea or two just waiting to be sprung.

Slate relief by Ann Jones.

Slate relief by Ann Jones.

Ann Jones in her studio.

Pine Scents

One often hears that the only pine needles with a good fragrance are those from the balsam pine. These are the strongest scented but certainly not the only ones. When they are dry any pine needles can easily be broken, which releases the wonderfully fresh smell. If there are pine trees, their needles can usually be found blanketing the woodland floor all summer. In the fall you can pick the dried needles from the trees in back yard areas as well. Pine needles can be used to make elegant little sachet "pillows" to keep drawers smelling sweet or to give as gifts. They can be made in any size or shape that you like. They are easy to make once you have gathered the fragrant pine needles. The pine needles can also be combined with dried flower petals and herbs.

The sachet pillows can be made from old-fashioned delicate printed fabric, pastel taffeta, calico, velvet, or by sewing different ribbons together to create your own fabric. Different widths of velvet ribbon combined with the wide elaborately designed ribbons often used for borders makes a unique "fabric". Be sure that the fabric you have chosen is not too thin so that the needles will not poke through it. The shape need not be square. Hearts, strawberries, or rose buds can be formed for an unusual sachet. If you'd rather not do any sewing, for a last-minute gift you can simply gather the corners of the fabric you are using and tie them together with a pretty ribbon. Insert a spring of pine or dried herb into the bow.

After picking or gathering the dried pine needles break them up into pieces that are not too large. Fill the ribbon or fabric pillow or spoon some into the center of the fabric. If you would like to combine the pine scent with an herb, you might try equal parts of rose geranium, or lemon verbena, lavender, or rosemary, with the pine.

Woodland Assemblages

Working with pieces of weathered wood to make an assemblage can be a real challenge. It is almost impossible to show you how, in step-by-step photographs and instructions because no two pieces of wood are exactly alike. There are many artists and crafts people working exclusively with driftwood and other interesting pieces of found materials. What you create depends largely on your own imagination. Sometimes the designs are abstract; others are realistic. The assemblages that are shown here were all made from pieces of found wood as well as utilizing twigs and pine cones. Fallen branches and dried bark can sometimes be designed into a piece and often resemble a realistic object.

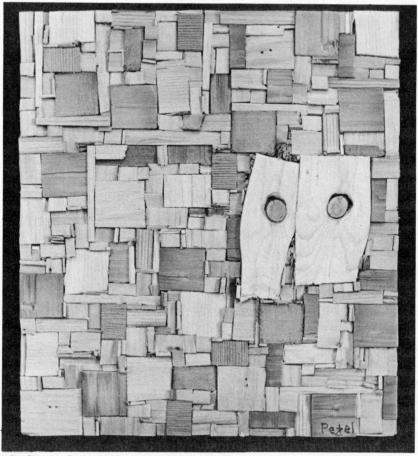

"Owl" wood assemblage by Henry Petzel.

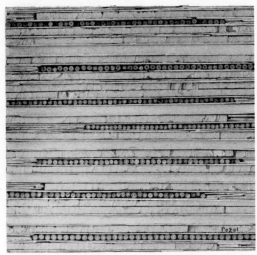

"Navaho," by Henry Petzel.

Detail of "Navaho" by Henry Petzel.

Henry Petzel is an accomplished artist who has won many prizes for his assemblages and collages. His inspiration comes from his surroundings. I asked Henry if he decides first what he will create and then goes out to seek the right odds and ends of material to put together. Quite the opposite. When out for a walk in the woods or visiting a local lumberyard or boatyard, Mr. Petzel picks up interesting odds and ends. After gathering the materials that appeal to him he looks them over to see what they might be used for. Sometimes an unusual piece suggests a theme, and everything else is built around this original piece. This was the case with the knotty pieces of wood that suggested the assemblage called "The Owl." This is a marvelous construction using different sizes of rectangular pieces of raw wood. Once the design is planned, each piece is glued onto a wood background using epoxy glue. Once dry, a frame can be bought or made to fit the "painting."

Another of Henry's wood assemblages is the "Navaho." The pieces of assembled wood and twigs represent a piece of woven material. While on a trip out West Mr. Petzel was impressed with the cloth woven by Indians and used this fabric as inspiration for his assemblage. When you are doing craftwork of this kind ideas for designs can come from unlikely places. Here pieces of flat thin layers of wood are separated by small round pieces of twigs that have been cut up and placed between the wood rows. Once all the pieces were glued to a background board they were painted white and pale yellow. This wood assemblage actually looks like soft textured fabric.

The plaice fish is a type of flounder that is quite popular on Nantucket Island where Henry Petzel lives. This became the inspiration for a pine cone creation. The body of the fish is made entirely of the pine cone scales that have been glued to a wood board which is then painted with gesso—a background cover found in art-supply stores. Acrylic paint could also be used. When asked if he paints the subject first so that he will know where to glue the pieces, Henry told me that he simply makes a rough sketch and then creates the picture as he goes along.

If you would like to try an assemblage using pine cones, here are a few hints to make the job easier. Pine trees are found around the country although the species vary in different areas. Any type of pine cone will work for these crafting projects. The pine cones begin to fall from the trees in late August and September. Sometimes they are dry enough so that you can simply pull the scales from the cones with your fingers. However, this is not always the case, and you may find you need clippers to free the scales. Any variety can be used to make an interesting assemblage. It's a good idea to collect more than you think you will need. That way you'll have some left to make a pine cone wreath later on. If you live in a city and cannot easily get to an area, such as a park, for collecting cones, many craft shops and mail-order houses sell them for your convenience.

The pine cones are freshest when they are closed. For easy clipping of the scales, place the cones in a 200° oven so that they will open up. This is also a good idea for drying out damp pine cones. If it is very warm and sunny, the sun will do the trick.

Years ago our ancestors used a knife to strip the scales from the pine cones. Most craftworkers today find that clippers are best for this purpose. Pliers are also occasionally used. When stripping the scales from the cone, work around the cone, row by row. This is easier than clipping the scales off at random. They will graduate in size which will give you a variety of sizes from one pine cone.

Before assembling the pine cone scales into an arrangement, it is best to make a pencil outline or sketch of an overall plan. If you are making a fish, first look around for other pieces of wood or oddments that might be used for the head, eye, fins, etc. The pieces can then be easily glued in place using a white glue such as Elmer's Glue-All, Sobo, or for more holding power an epoxy glue. It takes longer for the white glue to dry, but it is much easier to use as it will wash off your hands easily.

To preserve the design, you might consider spraying it with clear matte varnish, or glossy finish if you would like it to have a shiny surface. Once completed, the design can be finished with a painted background. This can be done with an acrylic paint or gesso that is applied around the object to cover any exposed surface. Make or purchase a suitable frame and your work is ready to be hung.

"The Plaice" made of pine cones by Henry Petzel.

Pressing Leaves

Autumn is, of course, the favorite time to collect leaves. You may be turning your attention to pine cone wreaths and drying gourds, but don't ignore the familiar leaves. The colors are so varied and when pressed will keep their colors so that you can use them in many crafting projects. It is best to pick freshly fallen leaves even if they are wet. When placed between two pieces of paper toweling the moisture will be absorbed. I find that vine leaves and long blades of grass are wonderful to have as ground cover for a natural collage or nature scene. Fill a page with grasses while you are at it. Ferns also press well, don't seem to change their color, and can be used in many crafting projects.

The best results are usually obtained if leaves are placed on several layers of newspaper. Do not have the leaves touch or overlap one another. Cover the layer of leaves with more newspaper and weight them down with heavy books. As the leaves are being pressed the newspaper will absorb excess moisture. Set this in a dark cool area, such as a basement or garage. If the leaves you are pressing are green, they should be pressed for about a month. If they have already turned in color, two weeks should be sufficient. If they are removed from the paper before they are completely dried out, the edges will curl. However, don't leave them longer than necessary or they will become brittle and will crack and break when handled. Dry more than you think you'll need, for they are marvelous background material.

Another method for drying some leaves, such as maple or coleus, is pressing them with a warm iron. Place a leaf between two pieces of waxed paper, set the iron on a low temperature, and press. The wax from the paper will melt and coat both sides of the leaf. Remove the leaf, let it cool, and press overnight in a book. You can do this with green grasses and ivy as well as the autumn leaves.

Leaf-it Box

Materials needed:
Assortment of fresh leaves
Heavy books for pressing
Newspaper
Glossy polymer medium (Grum-
  bacher, Weber, Palmer, are some
  brand names)

Iron
Paint brush ½- or 1-inch
Wet-or-Dry sandpaper #400
Clear paste wax (optional)
Cardboard, metal, or wood box
Razor blade

Using autumn leaves as a covering decoration for boxes, cans, even a trunk or suitcase can create an interesting effect. The leaves are such beautiful colors in the fall, and you can collect as many as you need to cover even the largest item in no time at all. You can even use green leaves for this project. Once the leaves have been used to cover the box, it will have a textured look but will be smooth to the touch because of the polymer coatings.

Coat each leaf with polymer medium and let dry.

Begin by pressing your leaves as described on page 39. Remove the leaves and one by one paint the underside with the polymer medium. This is a water-base varnish that will dry in five to ten minutes. (The brush can be rinsed clean with warm water.) This coating of the polymer medium will give the leaves body so that they will be easy to handle. The object that you choose to cover can be a wooden, cardboard, or metal box. A round oatmeal box might be used, or perhaps you have an old cannister. A hinged wooden box, obtainable in most craft shops could be lined with an interesting early American print once the box is covered. A recipe or file box is another possibility.

Begin by sanding the box so that it is smooth. If you are using a cardboard box, this step won't be necessary. However, it is a good idea to coat the box with polymer medium so that you will have a clean surface on which to work. After sanding a wooden or metal box, coat the top with polymer medium. This will act as your gluing agent. If you are using a cardboard box, wait until the first polymer medium coating is dry before applying another coat. Lay each leaf onto the wet surface. Do a section at a time, adding more polymer medium as you go along. Leaves should overlap to completely cover an entire section. Press the leaf down firmly with the palm of your hand. As you complete each section of the box, place a piece of newspaper on top of leaves and go over it with a warm iron. This will make the leaves adhere better. Be sure that there is no excess polymer medium on the top of the leaves or the newspaper will stick to the surface. Cover all exposed areas with leaves.

Set the box aside to dry for about an hour. With a safety razor blade make a slit all the way around the opening of the box where the top and bottom come together. Using the glossy polymer medium varnish, brush it over the entire box so that all the leaves are completely coated. This will dry in about ten min-

Apply more medium to each leaf before pressing it to the box.

utes. Apply several more coats so that the leaves become submerged under the medium. After six coats sand over all exposed surfaces using #400 Wet-or-Dry sandpaper. Apply another coat of varnish and let this dry before lining the box.

The lining can be done in several ways. Wrapping paper or wallpaper comes in a variety of designs that would contrast nicely with the leaf design. Felt or Contact paper can also be used as a lining. A map of your state is another possibility for this purpose. Measure all inside walls before cutting out each lining piece. Use the polymer medium to attach the paper inside the box. Contact paper has an adhesive backing, and Elmer's or Sobo glue is best for a felt lining. Paint the rim of the inside of a wooden box in a matching color and then coat the inside lining and painted rim with polymer medium. This will protect the lining as well as give it a shiny finish.

As a final touch, rub over the outside finish with a small piece of very fine, #0000 steel wool. Wipe away any particles and apply a thin coat of clear furniture paste wax.

Feathered Body Ornaments

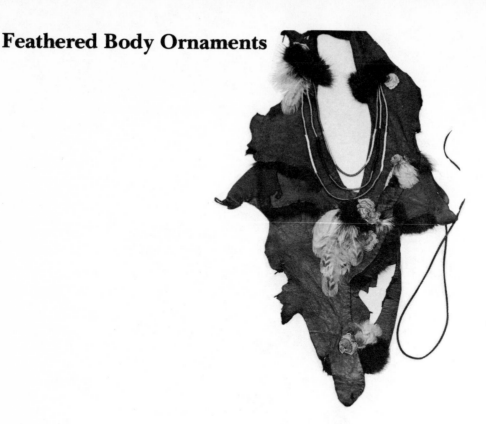

Beth Trudeau is an innovative craft designer who brings her enthusiasm for a variety of crafts to the children's art classes given in her studio. From the walls hang colored balls of yarn, dried milkweed, and sprigs of bittersweet. Wooden milk crates are bolted together and hung for shelving. Long low tables run the full length of both sides of the room. They are perfect for spreading out the materials when Beth is working. More cushioned milk crates are stored under the tables for easy access stools. In a closet she has cigar boxes labeled and stacked in more crates. Labels that read: "milkweed pods," "feathers," "shells," "coconut," are clues to some of the crafting projects done here.

One wall of the studio is used to display her beautifully designed feathered breast plates. At one time many local boutiques carried these unique body ornaments. Now Beth says she prefers to sell them herself. "That way I can design it for the individual. If a customer wants something that I've already made, I get more satisfaction from the direct contact of seeing it on the person. They tell me what they like. And often I can tell them what I think would look well. In this way my work is appreciated more. It's a personal involvement that is the nature of this particular craft."

Beth's crafting materials hang on her studio walls for inspiration.

Beth uses remnants of very soft leather for the basic material. Some are made with antelope; others, deerskin. The colors are lovely, warm shades of brown and natural.

Each body ornament is individually designed using feathers, bone, shells, fungus, and other natural material that Beth is attracted to. She spends a lot of time collecting the material in the areas around her house. There is a small wooded grove where she always finds something interesting to bring home. "My neighbors are beginning to wonder about me," she said. "For two years I've lived here and they've watched me come home with some very strange-looking objects." She pulled a log out from one of the crate shelves. "Sometimes a single log has as many as ninety pieces of poly pores on it. Aren't the colors beautiful?" The velvety textured, fan-shaped poly pores attached to the log had patterns of browns, grays, some pink and purple that were exquisitely subtle. "What you use for decoration is a very personal decision," Beth explained. "You should add the things that you feel compliment your own body or personality. The use of different textures is exciting."

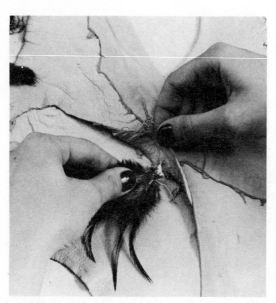

Rubber cement pieces of feathers and fungi under seams temporarily.

Poke hole in poly pores with a sharp instrument such as X-Acto blade.

Making a Body Ornament: Begin by holding odd-shaped scraps of the leather on your body to get the initial form. These pieces of leather can be purchased from a leather supply company, craft store, or you can buy a large piece in a fabric store and cut it up. Beth suggests the possibility of getting scraps from a garment manufacturer. These scraps might otherwise be thrown away.

Design the pieces so that they relate well to one another. You might want to begin by making the first project narrow, more like a necklace than an entire covering. Put dabs of contact cement where the pieces overlap. This will temporarily hold them together while you add the decoration. Remove the leather piece and place it on a work surface. The leather pieces will be handsewn together once you have secured the decorations.

The feathers and other ornaments are glued in place here and there by lifting up the overlapping edges of the leather. Sometimes Beth sews the feathers together before securing them to the leather. She also suggests taking a small piece of fabric, such as muslin, and gluing it over the tops of the feathers. In this way you can more easily sew them to the leather.

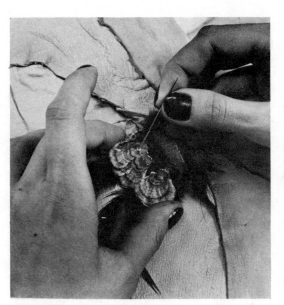

Sew poly pores in place.

Beth attaches the finishing touch to her feathered body ornament.

Glue each feather in place with a dot of contact cement for placement. If you don't like the way it looks, you can easily pull it off and place it elsewhere. The cement will not stain the leather. The poly-pore is placed on top of a piece of fur or feathers. This can be done by making holes in the top of the poly-pore. Use an X-Acto blade or other sharp instrument. You can then sew the poly-pore and the feathers to the leather. Use heavy-duty cotton thread in the color of the feathers.

Once all the decorations have been secured, hand-sew the pieces of leather together where the edges overlap. Beth then cuts out a piece of solid black material for the backing. This is hand-sewn to cover the rough edges and give the piece a finished look. A leather thong is attached to one side at the waist. A small loop is attached to the opposite side. Bring the thong around your back and tie through the loop. Cut off the excess. The thong will hold your body ornament in place when wearing.

These natural body ornaments are only part of what Beth makes. Everywhere you look in the studio and the rest of her home you find the evidence of her creative ability.

In the Fields

Whatever the season my favorite place to take a walk is a big open field. There is always something worthwhile waiting to be discovered. And such variety! Aside from the visual treat are the smells. Of course what you find in a field depends on what part of the country you live in. However, the variety of wildflowers, vines, grasses, etc. is so great in the United States that there is no way on earth that a field trip won't yield an abundance of treats. Many of the plants, particularly wildflowers, that are found in fields are also seen along roadsides and in vacant lots. While you will miss out on some of the extra things that happen when wandering in fields, the flowers are still available even if you don't have access to fields.

Wildflowers grow almost everywhere, and in some parts of the country there are always some in bloom. Many states maintain their roadside wildflowers and it is not a good idea to hop out of your car, scissors in hand, every time you see some beauties you'd like to take home. As with many of our natural resources we once thought flowers to be unlimited. In some areas the wildflowers have been greatly over picked, and therefore many states list the flowers that are becoming scarce and should not be taken. State parks usually prohibit flower gathering. Check before wandering into a field in an area with which you aren't familiar. The chamber of commerce will give you this information. And please be sure to take only a limited number from one area, not depleting a certain area of a particular flower.

Most wildflowers are considered weeds and usually grow in the poorest soil and under the worst conditions. One of my favorites is chicory which is usually found in sandy, dry waste places. By itself, one lone chicory is not exceptionally pretty. The color, however, is an exquisite blue, like lilac, and when you come upon a field of chicory, usually growing near the seashore, it is breathtaking. All that blue! Chicory is often the sole inhabitant of a vacant lot or abandoned doorway area. It is best to enjoy the chicory right where it is. Once picked it will not last long. When pressed it becomes too delicate to handle and loses its color entirely. So enjoy it in its natural environment when you come upon it.

Fields of Queen Anne's lace are just as beautiful, if a bit more subtle. These are very common by the wayside and in dry fields, blossoming from July through September. This lacelike weed is often deemed a great pest by farmers. Sometimes referred to as wild carrot, this weed is particularly abundant in the Northeast. Gather lots of it. You can press it easily, dry it, use it in arrangements, embed it under candle wax, to list a few crafting ideas.

As for me, I'll take the buttercup or lowly dandelion over all the other wildflowers any day. Buttercups are such a delightful surprise when you come upon them growing in little clumps here and there. Did anyone from your childhood ever come up with a negative response to that buttercup test, do you like butter? Buttercups are by far the best flower to press and use for collages, flower arrangements under glass, or combined with decoupage. When handled carefully they are quite easy to work with. The petals alone are terrific combined with other flower parts to create "flower characters" and the stems can be curved and pressed for graceful arrangements. The leaves are also interesting and press well.

During the summer between mowings my lawn looks like dandelion haven. Each day I pick a large bunch, put them in a small white vase and place it on my kitchen window sill. They don't last long, but each summer morning offers a whole new crop. I never press or dry dandelions. I simply enjoy them. As for crafting with dandelions, they can be used while in bloom or in their feathery seed-globe state.

Wildflower gardening has become popular in recent years. Even in a city apartment it doesn't take much space to maintain a small variety of wildflowers. Before planting your wildflower seeds get an inexpensive guide book, such as one from the Golden Nature Series, to check out the details of a flower's natural habitat, whether it should grow in sun or shade, soil conditions, and other information about the plant and its region. Wildflower gardens don't need too much attention because of the nature of the plant, and growing them yourself you'll not only have the special joy of watching them grow, but a steady supply for your craft projects.

Besides wildflowers, berries and leaves can be gathered in the fields. Honeysuckle vines, long grasses, and burrs are some of nature's offerings for craft projects. Collect odds and ends of things even if you don't know what they are or where you might use them. Once spread before you on your work table they will spark an idea and the more you have the more possibilities you will have to choose from.

When gathering in the fields wear work boots and take along gloves to protect your hands. A large shopping bag and clippers are also handy.

Pressing Flowers

I have recently gone "pressed-flower crazy." When the first blooms of spring started to pop out in a haphazard direction, I started picking. I didn't know exactly what I would do with the flowers once pressed, but I knew one thing for sure. I was going to use them in any crafting project that could possibly incorporate a pressed flower. I was amazed how well the flowers could be preserved, and now that it is fall I am having such fun opening papers and finding spring buttercups and daisies. From my experience and observation, I have found that some flowers press better than others. The color retention is best, for example, in yellow flowers such as buttercups and daffodils. Pink dogwood blossoms also retain their color. The blues usually turn pale pink or beige, and the reds turn to brown. When selecting flowers to be pressed choose those in full bloom as well as the buds, leaves, and even some flowers that have been slightly damaged. These can be used for the petals for stems and leaves.

It is easiest to press naturally flat flowers such as the pansy, but it is not necessary to limit yourself to these. Flowers that press well include the black-eyed Susan, cosmos, daisy, heather, lavender, Queen Anne's lace, tansy, and zinnia, to name a few. Try whatever strikes your fancy; you may find it works well. It is very easy to press flowers. There are variations, but basically the procedures are the same no matter what the flower. Some people prefer to use newspaper rather than blotting paper, or a press as opposed to using books. The following method is what works best for me.

Begin by cutting up white blotting paper into pieces approximately 8 x 11 inches. Using the corregated boxes that you find in supermarkets, cut them into pieces the same size as the blotting paper. The boxes can be cut apart with a matte knife or a safety-edge razor blade. Place several flowers and leaves on a piece of the blotting paper so that they do not overlap. Each page can be filled with as many flowers as can comfortably fit. Place another piece of blotting paper on top of the page of flowers and over this place one of the corregated boards. Repeat this procedure until you have a stack of six to ten layers. Place the stack of sandwiched flowers on a solid surface and pile several heavy books on top of the pile. If you prefer and have some bricks handy, they can be used rather than the books. This method of pressing is a good way to press a large quantity of flowers at one time. If, however, you would like to simply press one page of flowers, you can lay the flowers between two pieces of paper toweling and place between two pages of a very heavy book. With the book on a table put a few more books on top to weight it down.

Pressed flowers should be left for a minimum of one week,

but if you have the time it is better to wait two weeks before using them. The blotting paper or toweling absorbs the moisture in the flowers as they dry out. Once the moisture is completely absorbed, the flowers will be brittle and should be handled carefully. When using them in craft projects it is good to have a tweezer handy for easy lifting and placing.

Decorator Tiles

Materials needed:
Four solid-color bathroom tiles   *Tweezers (optional)*
Polymer medium or white glue   *Spray varnish*
Sponge brush   *Tile adhesive*
Cuticle scissors   *Heavy cardboard*

Since decorated tiles are so expensive and often hard to find in unique designs I thought making them myself with pressed flowers might be fun. This is a good first project that will give you practice in using pressed flowers to create a design before perhaps going on to making a pressed-flower collage on canvas. These tiles, once decorated, can be framed and hung in the kitchen. You might make them into a square pattern or you

Plan a design and lay the pressed flowers on the tile.

could frame each one separately. I also like them when arranged side by side above the sink or window frame. Each tile can be designed as an individual scene, or the flowers can create a complete design when all four tiles are together. If you will be using them together, the tiles should be laid side by side when working so that the design will flow from one to the other.

The tiles that I used are inexpensive bathroom tiles purchased in a building-supply/hardware store. Any solid color can be used. I chose white because the flowers and leaves tend to show up best on a white background.

Begin by preparing the tiles. Each one should be washed with soap and water so that the surface is absolutely clean. Dry thoroughly. Select the pressed flowers and leaves that you will be using. It is fun to spread the pressed material before you and

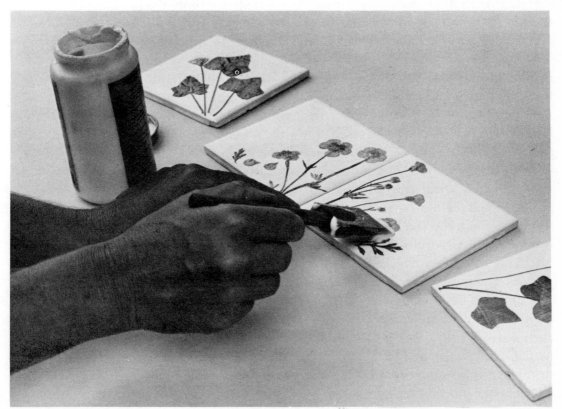

Apply polymer medium over the flowers to protect them.

begin arranging and rearranging different combinations. If you need an extra leaf on something, cut it from somewhere else and add it to your arrangement. Cuticle scissors are best for trimming and piecing bits here and there. They are tiny and easy to work with when cutting the delicate stems and buds. Try several flowers on each tile until you feel that the design is right. By "right" I mean what looks good to *you*. There is no rule to follow. It should just be pleasing from your point of view. If you have pressed a large enough variety, you can match the flower colors to your room color. If not, most wildflowers fit in anywhere. For this project I used buttercups and ivy.

When you know where the materials will be placed, take them off the tiles being sure to handle them with care. I used a matte finish polymer medium to attach the flowers. This is a water-soluble varnish that is available in craft and art-supply stores. It is thinner than glue and can be brushed evenly over the tile surface. Or you can thin regular white glue with water and brush it over the tile before placing the flowers in position. The polymer medium or glue will be clear when dry. Using tweezers to lift each flower and leaf is the easiest way to handle them. Place the pieces one at a time in the desired place on the wet tile. Tap them down securely with the tweezer or a brush handle. Do not touch the pressed flowers with your fingers. If there is any glue on your hands or on the flower when you touch it, the piece will stick to your finger and lift off. They are very delicate. Once the materials of your design have been applied to all the tiles, they should be left to dry for about thirty minutes. Then dip the brush into the polymer medium so that it is very wet. Carefully dab the brush over the flowers on each tile. This will give each design a protective coating. It will appear as a white foam when the polymer is first applied, but it will dry to a clear matte finish. This should be left to dry for another twenty minutes. Once dry you can spray each tile with a clear varnish in the finish of your choice. The matte finish will be flat with no shine. The glossy finish will be very shiny when dry. Either finish is quite nice. For my project I used the matte, which is like a satin finish.

Each coat of varnish will take a full day or overnight to dry completely. Three coats of varnish should be the minimum that you apply. If you are planning to use this as a trivet, you will want to keep reapplying the varnish until the designs are completely submerged and the surface is smooth to the touch. This could take as many as twenty coatings of varnish. Once you have several coats on the tiles the varnish will begin to dry faster and you will be able to apply as many as three coats of spray varnish each day. While drying, place the tiles out of the way to avoid dust particles settling in the varnish. Do not sand between coats as this will ruin the design. Place each tile on top of heavy cardboard or illustration board backing in the way you want the finished project to look. With a pencil draw a line around the tiles. Remove the tiles and cut out the board with a razor blade or matte knife. Use a ruler as a guide to draw the blade against.

Spread the back of each tile with tile adhesive or tile grout, as well as all edges of the tiles that will butt against one another. This adhesive (there are many brands) can be purchased in a hardware store. Place each tile at the corners of the paper. Push the tiles together so that they all touch and the edges meet. If there is excess backing around the outer edges of the tile this can be trimmed later. Set this aside to dry for several hours. Read the directions of the adhesive tube for the exact drying time. Once dry, you can use your razor blade to trim the excess backing.

The tiles can now be mounted on a wall in several ways. 3M Scotch brand mounting squares are self-sticking adhesives that can be placed on each corner of the backing and pressed against the wall. A self-adhering cloth picture hanger can be attached to the center back. Or you can measure the outside width and height and purchase a frame to set the tiles in. I like to keep mine on the counter lying flat so they can be used as a large trivet. You might want to add a piece of felt to the cardboard backing to finish off the project and to help protect your table top.

Wild Cards

Materials needed:
Blank cards with envelopes
Clear plastic Contact paper ½ yard
Felt-tip marker
Scissors

Making your own greeting cards with pressed-flower decorations is a wonderful way to remember a special occasion. If you have a supply of pressed flowers available, you can whip up a card any time. If you happen to know the names and are familiar with the flowers, it is a special touch to send a birthday card decorated with the flower of that month. These cards are fun to make and take absolutely no special crafting skills.

I have often used blank Strathmore cards because the paper is quite lovely, the size is good, and they come in a variety of colors. Also, each has a matching envelope. If you cannot find these cards in art-supply stores, you can make your own cards with colorful paper. Choose paper that is not too flimsy, such as construction paper, and cut the size card that you would like. Be sure to first check envelope sizes so that you aren't stuck with an unusual size for which there is no envelope.

Select a few pressed flowers, leaves, grasses, etc. that will look well together. It is not necessary to fill the entire space. Sometimes a simple stem with a single bud can look quite elegant. An arrangement of leaves against a rust-colored background would be nice for a fall celebration.

Place the elements on the blank card. Cut a piece of the clear plastic Contact paper so that it is slightly larger than the card front. Peel the backing away from the Contact and place the self-adhesive paper on top of the flowers. The Contact paper should extend out a bit all the way around the edge of the card. Press the Contact paper down so that it will adhere to the card and flowers or leaves, etc. With a wooden pencil roll over the Contact so that any air bubbles will smooth out. Trim the outer edges with your scissors or a razor blade. Open the card and with a felt marker of a contrasting color write your message.

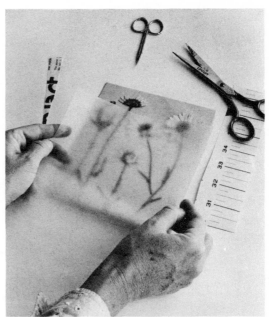

Pressed daisies are carefully placed on the front of the card. No glueing is necessary. Cover the flowers with clear Contact paper. Wild card takes minutes to make.

Wedding Announcement

Materials Needed:
Wedding announcement
Plastic box frame
Colored paper
Rubber cement
Elmer's glue
Pressed flowers
Razor blade
Straight edge (such as a ruler with
  a metal edge)
Pencil and ruler
A push pin
Tracing paper
Two feet of 1" wide grosgrain ribbon

A personalized wedding invitation, birth, or anniversary announcement can be framed and designed for a lasting gift. If you have been pressing a variety of flowers, you might even have the exact flower of the month. However, as long as you have some delicate flowers and grasses you can begin right away. If not, you start by pressing flowers and leaving them for at least a week. (See Pressing Flowers, page 51.)

The wedding invitation that I used is 4 ½ × 6 ¼ inches, and the frame is 5 × 7 inches. However, the plastic frames come in larger sizes and you might prefer this. Measure your invitation or announcement before selecting the frame. The 8 × 10-inch size is probably best for most cards. The backing paper can be anything you want. There are all kinds of possibilities as well as colors. You might like to have a shiny paper or even a delicate fabric for the background.

Use an oversized piece of paper for the background so that you do not have to be overly concerned with placement. Positioning does not have to be perfect because you will cut the paper to size after the invitation is mounted.

 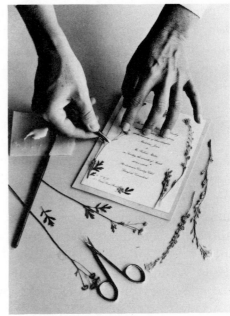

Put pin in corner of each penciled outline. *Design with small flowers.*

Using a razor blade and a straight edge, cut away the front of the invitation so that you are left with a single piece of paper to be mounted. To attach the invitation to the background, coat the back with rubber cement, available from art-supply stores. Coat the front of the background paper also and let both pieces of paper dry separately. Unlike gluing with Elmer's, you do not make contact until the gluing agent is dry. If you don't wait, it will not stick properly. When the rubber cement is thoroughly dry place the invitation on top of the background paper. Carefully place another piece of clean paper, such as tracing or typing paper, on top of the invitation and rub firmly over the top of the paper. This paper protection will prevent any dirt or finger marks from getting on the invitation.

Measure the inside of the frame you will be using. On a separate piece of tracing paper measure and draw that size rectangle. Position the tracing paper over the invitation so that it is straight and centered. You can do this by eye. With a push pin, make a little hole in each corner right through to the background paper or matte board. Remove the pin and tracing paper. To cut out the rectangle around the invitation, place your ruler between the holes and hold a razor ar X-Acto knife against it. You should hold the tool straight up and down to avoid cutting a crooked edge. If you are using matte board as the background, don't try to cut through on the first cut. Go over the lines three times. In this way you will not have a jagged edge and you will avoid cutting your fingers.

It is best not to glue the flowers to the paper. They are quite delicate and the glue tends to stain them. The pressure of the cardboard backing of the frame will usually hold the flowers in place, but not always. As a precaution against that possibility, I suggest designing and applying the flowers this way. First select and tentatively place the pressed material around the invitation. They can overlap from the background paper onto the edges of the card. This softens the hard edge. If you are using a larger frame, thus a larger background, there is more space for placement. Try several different arrangements before settling on the final one. Large flowers tend to look heavy while the smaller and lighter-colored ones are delicate. A baby announcement might be decorated with tiny buds.

Once you have made a final decision, you can attach each piece with a tiny spot of glue placed on the back of each flower. Just dot the glue on the stem and flower head in strategic places so that it will adhere to the paper. Press the flower down and try to touch it as little as possible. When all the flowers are in place set the project aside to dry for approximately half an hour.

Lay the decorated invitation on top of the cardboard insert that comes with the frame and place the plastic frame on top of this. It should fit snuggly. If you want to finish off the edges a ribbon border can be placed around the cardboard insert before placing it into the frame. I used 1″ pink and white checked grosgrain ribbon to match the background. There are holes on the back of the insert that have been prepunched for framing, so it is now ready to give and hang. If you want to, you can sign your name on the back with a felt-tip pen.

Leaded-glass Flower Box

When I first saw handcrafted stained glass boxes and terrariums I was quite impressed. I had always associated stained glass only with windows. Many talented glass crafters today do create stained-glass windows, but the art medium also includes smaller projects that can be done in a relatively short period of time.

Craig Kay is a self-taught stained-glass craftworker. His beautifully designed windows, mirrors, lamps, terrariums, and

Antique glass box by Craig Kay.

Materials needed:
*3 pieces of 8 × 10-inch window-
    pane or antique stained glass*
Glass cutter
One roll of ⅜-inch copper-foil tape
60 - 40 solid core solder
2 ounces copper sulfate
Paste flux
Brush
80–150 watt soldering iron

Lubricating oil or kerosene
Sponge
Felt-tip pen
⅛-inch copper tubing
Ruler
Pliers
Medium-grit sandpaper (#200)
l8-gauge copper wire
Pressed flowers of your choice
Fine steel wool

Craig Kay working in his stained-glass studio.

boxes reflect a love of nature. Craig takes his design ideas from his natural environment, and most of what he does has a light, airy quality much like the material itself. When I first saw Craig working in his studio I thought that the amateur craftworker could never learn to make a glass project. But Craig assured me that with clear instructions and the right materials almost any-one could create a simple box. Once the technique is learned, you will be able to make pressed-flower window hangings, pend-ants, even small terrariums. All the materials are available in craft shops and if there is not a well-stocked store in your area, you will find mail-order sources at the end of this book. (Believe it or not, you can actually order glass through the mail.) Craig's boxes have incorporated feathers and leaves as well as seashells mounted on top and flowers sandwiched between two layers of glass.

The box that Craig has made is 4 × 4 inches square. It is a useful size and not difficult to handle. When you become more experienced you may want to try larger or more unusual shapes. The bottom of this box is made with mirrored glass and the top is a beveled piece. These pieces can be purchased pre-cut. You can also use the clear glass for the top and bottom as well as sides.

Before cutting the glass spread a layer of newspaper on a clean work surface. Clean the glass with Windex or similar glass cleaner before cutting. An inexpensive glass cutter can be purchased in a hardware store or craft shop. Soak a small piece of sponge in household lubricating oil or kerosene. Drop this into the bottom of a small jar and rest the cutter on it in the bottle. This will keep it lubricated. The cutter should be oiled after each cut.

When measuring the pieces for the box it is best if you can cut one long 4″ high piece for all the sides. Then cut your pieces from this so that all four sides are the same height. Craig used a piece of glass that was 5 × 16 inches. This may be difficult to find, however, and you may be forced to use the 8 × 10-inch sheets, measuring out your 4-inch squares for the sides, top and bottom. Mark the measure with a felt-tip pen. One of the sides will be a double piece because the flowers will be sandwiched

To cut the glass: A metal ruler or T square will be useful in order to cut a straight line. Start at the edge and make a very smooth definite cut in one continuous motion. Apply pressure as you do this. The cutter will scratch through the surface of the glass and weaken it at this point. With thumbs on either side of the score, firmly press and break it in half. If the edges are a little rough sand with sandpaper to smooth slightly. Clean the edges of the glass with Windex once all the pieces are cut.

Select your pressed flowers and arrange them on one piece of glass. Place the slightly smaller (3¾") piece of glass on top so that the pressed flowers are between the two layers. Apply the copper foil around the four edges taping the two glass pieces together. Press it down on all edges. Run the copper foil around the edges of the other pieces of glass. Press down the copper foil on all edges and use a wooden pencil to flatten the

Hold the glass cutter straight up and down to make a clean cut.

*Hold glass firmly on either side of the cut line and press with your
thumbs to snap the glass in half.*

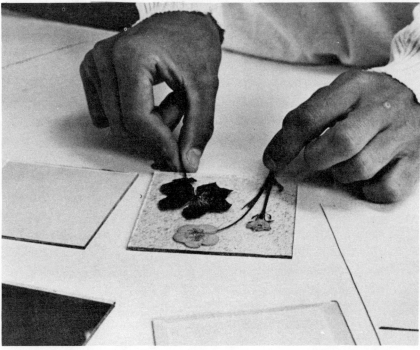

Arrange flowers on one piece of the glass.

tape. Run the side of the pencil along all edges to be sure that all copper foil is smooth and secure.

All edges of the glass must be wrapped, as the copper gives the lead something to grip onto. The solder will not stick to the glass alone. Therefore, if when soldering, some liquid gets on the glass, it will be easy to remove.

Hold the four pieces together to form the walls of the box. If you use masking tape to hold them together, you will find that it is easier to handle than simply balancing them while lining up the sides. Place the taped box on top of a piece of paper and draw a pencil line around the outside. Make sure the box is perfectly square. Lay a piece of clear glass on top of this and mark the lines with the felt pen. Cut two pieces this size for the top and bottom. If you have a precut mirrored piece for the bottom and another piece of glass for the top, this step can be eliminated.

Decide which way the box will open and select a piece to be hinged. The hinge will be made from the 18-gauge copper

Place another cut piece of glass over the pressed flower.

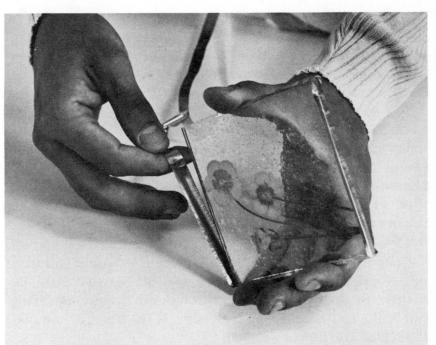

All edges of glass must have self-sticking copper foil over them.

The unassembled pieces for the glass box.

wire. Take a piece off the roll. It should extend 1½″ on each side of the glass. Straighten the wire with a hammer. Cut this piece off using pliers. Rub the wire with steel wool or sandpaper to allow the solder to stick to it. Hold the wire up to the side of the box to check the length.

The wire for the hinge must roll freely in a tube in order to work. This tube is called the barrel and can be purchased in a hobby store, or you can make it quite easily. Cut two pieces of copper foil the same size as the back of the top piece of glass. Leave the backing on the foil. Roll this foil around the piece of wire. This will create a barrel. Take the second piece of foil, remove the backing and wrap it around the first piece, covering the seam. Press it down all the way around forming a tube.

Craig uses an 80-watt Weller soldering iron with a temperature control. However, if your iron does not have a control, he suggests unplugging it often so that it doesn't get too hot. This can be done after soldering each edge. If the iron gets too hot, the solder won't stick.

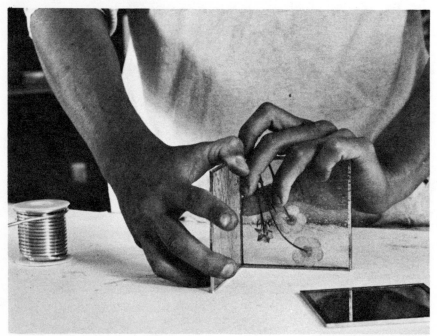

Assemble the glass pieces upside down so that the top of the box will line up perfectly.

Solder the outside of all seams of the box.

Before soldering use the flux to paint all copper surfaces inside and out. This is a lubricant for the solder. It is available in craft stores as well as hardware stores. Use a small paint brush to apply this. Heat the soldering iron for about ten minutes. The solder comes on a roll and looks like wire. Line up two sides of the box corner to corner. Assemble the box upside down so that any deviation in the glass size will be on the bottom. To hold the sides in place tack solder at the corner edges with a spot of solder. This can be done by holding the end of the solder against the edge of the box and touching the tip of the hot iron against the solder. It will drop a bead or glob of solder on the spot. Once the sides have a drop of solder to hold them, check to be sure that the top fits squarely and flat on the top of all four sides. Line up all bottom corners and tack solder at each corner. Solder the inside seams first. Hold the tip of the iron to the solder on the inside of the box drawing a bead up the seam. If it does not stick to the copper, more flux may be needed. If there are bumps or bubbles, run the hot soldering iron over the area adding a bit of solder to smooth it out. Wipe the tip of the iron on a damp sponge frequently. Once the inside seams are soldered together draw a bead of solder up each outside seam of copper. While solder looks as though it will run or drip, it dries immediately on contact. However, be careful not to let the hot solder drip on your hands.

Secure hinge to top: Keep the seam of the hinge on the inside so it is covered and locked into the solder. Apply the flux all the way around the copper barrel (that you have made or bought) heating the solder as you apply it to the copper.

With 1½ inches of wire extended on either side of the barrel, use pliers to bend the side pieces down against the back side seams. Solder these pieces to the side seams. If you tack solder first, you will get it just right by moving the lid around slightly. Fiddle with the side hinges so that the lid fits well. Apply enough solder to completely cover the hinges. The solder dries and hardens almost on contact.

A matte knife can be used to clean off the excess solder once it is dry. Sand the edges so that there are no rough spots. A file

Solder the inside of all seams.

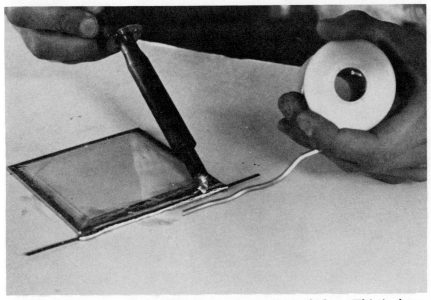

Solder a strip of wire along the back of one piece of glass. This is the hinge for the top of the box.

may be needed for this. Run fine steel wool over all edges to smooth them. Give the seams a good rubbing all around with steel wool.

To finish the box: Clean it in hot soapy water. Wash off the flux but be careful to do it quickly because the seams are not water-proof. A small scrub brush or old toothbrush may be helpful for scrubbing away dirt and grime. Dry it thoroughly with a soft towel.

To darken the leading: Boil a cup of water and add one tea-spoon of copper sulphate powder. It is a good idea to wear rub-ber gloves when mixing up the sulphate powder. Rub this mix-ture all over leaded seams with an old paint brush. The color of the lead changes to dark copper immediately. If the color doesn't change right away, it means that the water isn't hot enough. Go over all the seams several times. Do not get this on your clothing as it will discolor them. Dry the entire box when finished. Clean the glass with Windex.

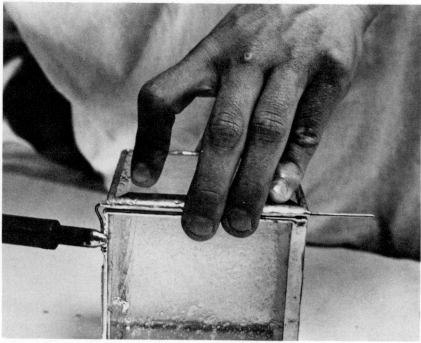

Solder hinge to side seams.

*Pressed flowers under glass can be hung
in a window or around your neck.*

Carol Anderson.

Hanging glass terrarium by Craig Kay.

*A pressed flower is soldered between two pieces of glass. A crocheted
chain will finish this off so that it can be worn as a neckpiece.*

Pressed-flower and Leaf Collage

Materials needed:
Hypro Stretchtite canvas 4 x 6-inch
Sky blue acrylic paint
White acrylic paint
Polymer varnish medium
Clear spray varnish (glossy finish)
Paint brush ½-inch
Scissors
Pressed flowers and blades of grass

Creating a painting from natural materials allows you the freedom to compose a scene without any knowledge of drawing. It is often a spontaneous act that begins with a bud or blade of grass and simply develops into something that one can be proud to display. Often you can't decide beforehand what you will make because the pressed materials seem to take over and do the designing for you. If you start out with a good selection of lovely well-pressed flowers, you can't miss. Leaves and blades of grass are nice for ground cover, and if you are creating a realistic scene, you might want to cover the stems of the flowers at the bottom.

I used the Hypro Stretchtite canvas available in art-supply stores. This paper canvas comes in a package of three and folds on scored lines to become a self-hanging boxed canvas. It does not, however, really look finished without a frame. Although it is paper, it has the texture of canvas and is good to paint on. This product is made by Grumbacher. If you prefer, you can use illustration board. This is also available in art-supply stores and comes in single and double weight.

On a piece of paper mix together a drop of blue paint with enough white paint to create a very pale blue color. A palette knife is excellent for mixing paint colors, but not necessary. Be sure to blend the paint so that it is smooth and the color consistent. The acrylic paint can be thinned with water if it seems too thick to spread easily. A ½-inch natural-hair brush is perfect for painting the canvas. Be sure that all areas are covered including the sides. Set this aside to dry for about twenty minutes. Clean the brush in warm water.

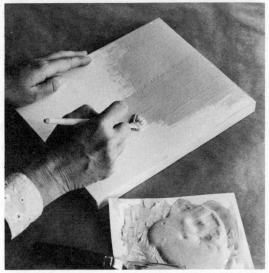

Decide which flowers and other materials you will include in your picture. Curved, graceful stems always soften a flower; sometimes they have been pressed this way. Choose colors that will look well against the background of "sky." You may want to add petals that will seem as though they are falling from the flower. I never hesitate to combine elements that don't naturally go together. Sometimes I press flowers at different times of the year or from different areas, and I find that the way things look or work together is the most important consideration.

Roughly plan what you will use before you begin. Check to see if the canvas is dry, then use your paint brush to apply a coat of polymer medium over the entire area. This will protect the background as well as act as a gluing agent for the flowers. When spread onto the blue paint it will appear to be murky white, but it does dry clear. Start with the largest flowers, filling in with the smaller ones. Place a flower down on the medium and tap it down lightly with the brush handle. Add elements one by one to create the rest of the design. The polymer medium dries very quickly, so keep reapplying it to the areas where you are about to place something. Stop and look over what you have done. There isn't any reason to rush through, so take all the time you need to decide how you want the composition to develop.

If you would like to add details, such as a butterfly or a specific color flower that you don't have, you can cut it out of paper. Thumb through some flower or butterfly books. There are inexpensive paperbacks with excellent color illustrations available in most book stores. Using cuticle scissors cut out what you need. Simply place it in the appropriate spot using the polymer medium to attach it to the canvas. Try not to touch the dried flowers any more than necessary because they tend to be quite fragile. When the design is complete hold it about twelve inches in front of you and apply a coat of clear acrylic spray varnish. This does not smell terrific, so do it where you have good ventilation. Even while drying the odor is not pleasant, so if you can put the collage in an out-of-the-way place to dry, it will help. It should take a couple of hours to dry thoroughly. Once dry repeat the spray coating. You may even want to reapply the varnish a third time so that the dried material is completely protected.

The back of the Stretchtite canvas has perforated holes for hanging, or you might find a suitable frame for your collage. If the frame is made of wood, it can be stained or painted in a color that will go with the collage. A moss-green or dark earth tone might look well next to the pale blue background.

Flowering Candles

Materials needed:
White candles (cylindrical)
Clear parafin wax
Pressed flowers
Baking pan
Paper towel
Tweezers

Candles that have been decorated with pressed flowers and leaves are especially lovely. The flowers appear to have been embedded in the candle but are simply placed on the outer surface with a protective wax covering. Arrange the flowers so that you have some delicate ones next to a heavier flower. Perhaps a leaf or two might look nice coming from the top. Pale colors create a delicate effect, but the brighter yellow or lilac colors show up best. Even when placed in a random pattern the flowers tend to look as though they are growing quite naturally. I like to add a few blades of grass to a flower scene.

Begin this project by pressing a variety of flowers and grass blades. If you are using some pulpy flower buds, after they are pressed you might want to iron them between pieces of brown paper to flatten them as much as possible. If it is the middle of winter and you have been pressing and storing flowers all spring and summer, now is the time for some surprises. It is always such fun to open those pressing papers and to discover a dogwood or daisy. I never label my sealed flowers because I like the surprise of discovery. It isn't as much fun to know beforehand what is inside. Of course, if I am looking for one specific flower or leaf this can be a problem, but I rather like it that way. Have enough material on hand so that you can do several candles at one time. It doesn't take much time or effort and is just as easy to do two or more while you have the wax melted.

The brightest colored flowers seem to work best for this project, as I have found that the wax coating will dull the color a bit. However, the white Queen Anne's lace is very elegant against a white candle even though the color seems to blend into the background.

Large, fat dripless candles work best for this project. The flame burns down through the center of the candle and the wax does not drip down the sides. As the flame gets lower and lower each time you burn the candle, it will create a glow from behind the flowers. So the more the candle is used, the prettier it is.

Begin by melting a cube of paraffin on the stove. This is clear, inexpensive wax that can be found in hardware stores or in the supermarket. There are usually four cubes to a package. A round cake pan is perfect for melting the wax. With your

82

Roll the surface of one side of the candle in the hot wax before placing flowers onto that side.

fingertips, hold the candle on either end and touch part of the candle to the surface of the hot wax. Do only one section at a time, but work quickly because the paraffin begins to cool immediately. Lift a flower with a tweezer and place it onto the candle where the hot wax has made contact. Press it in place using the tweezer to tap it down carefully. If the paraffin begins to cool before you can add all the flowers to the candle dip it into the hot paraffin again. Keep dipping and adding flowers to the candle. When all the flowers are on the candle hold either end and roll it over the surface of the hot wax so that the flowers are coated. The candle should not be submerged. Only the surface should touch the wax. Do this quickly to avoid a wax build-up. The quicker you do this, the smoother the candle surface will be.

Another method is to dip an old paint brush into the hot wax

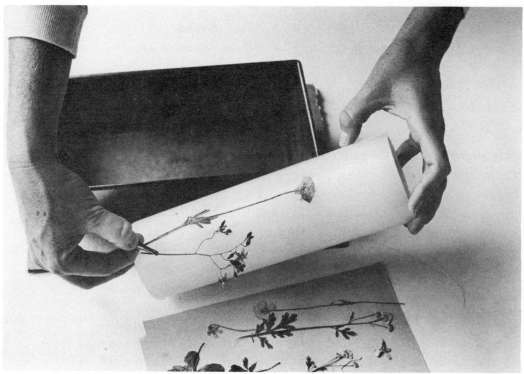

Quickly lay the chosen flowers onto the hot-wax surface of the candle. Tweezers make handling the flowers easier.

and brush it over the candle surface. Lay the flowers on the wax and coat another layer of wax over this, again using the paint brush. I prefer the rolling method, but you might try both. If you have a deep enough pan, you might also try filling it with paraffin and dipping the candle. I don't do it this way because you can create more drips on the outside, and it requires much more paraffin than you will need for the coating.

When you are finished place the pan of paraffin in the refrigerator. The paraffin will return to a solid state and can be easily removed so that you can use it again. You might like to pour it into a small can while it is hot. When hard it can be stored in the can. Or you might like to use it to make your own candles.

This is an easy, inexpensive gift to make or last-minute centerpiece for a holiday table.

Flowering Trays

Material needed:

Square tray, any size

Piece of glass cut to size of bottom inside

Several pressed flowers

Piece of fabric slightly larger than tray (or)

Lacy handkerchief

Pastel-colored matte board

Glue

Acrylic paint for tray

Small brush

Piece of #400 sandpaper

It is almost impossible today to find a lovely wooden bed tray. Could it be that nobody gets served in bed anymore? I really did try desperately to find one and can only say that if you have one, you are very lucky. Now's the time to do the most with it, even if you probably will be serving from it rather than being served with it. If you don't have a bed tray, any rectangular tray will do. The one I used is a lovely antique one that is quite small. To decorate a tray with wildflowers and then carry your breakfast to a quiet spot is like having a garden of your own any time you please. A lacy handkerchief or delicate flower-printed fabric is a beautiful background for a flower design. Or you may choose a solid pale pink or blue paper against which to show off the pressed violets or wild rose petals or delicate ferns.

If you want to paint the tray (whether it is metal or wood) use an acrylic paint. The colors are usually very vibrant and should be toned down with white paint. Use only a drop of color to create a pale pastel. Mix the paint evenly and paint all exposed areas of the tray. Let this dry for approximately half an hour. When the paint is thoroughly dry sand lightly with fine grit sandpaper such as #400.

Measure the inside of the tray bottom and cut a piece of glass (such as clear windowpane glass) to fit inside the tray. If you don't feel confident enough to cut the glass yourself, take the tray to a glass cutter. This is not expensive. Some hardware stores will cut glass to order.

Use this same measure to cut out a piece of paper. The paper can be placed in the bottom of the tray. You might place a lacy handkerchief on the paper and arrange the pressed flowers on top of this. Lay the glass carefully on top of the arrangement so that it will be held in place. For my blue tray I used heavy paper

Handle the pressed flowers carefully when laying them in place.

Small delicate pressed flowers will design well on this tray.

and did not glue the flowers down so that I could change my arrangement whenever I wanted to. If you decide to place the flowers directly on the board, they can be glued to it carefully with a tiny bit of white glue before placing the glass on top. When you want to change the arrangement you can then remove the entire paper and begin again. A border of grosgrain ribbon in a bright color can be added. Cut pieces of ribbon to the exact size of the bottom inside of the tray. Cut the corners so that they are mitered on the diagonal. Place the glass on top of the entire scene, ribbon and all.

If you would like to have a fabric background, cover the paper with a delicately printed design. Cut the paper so that it is approximately ⅛ inch smaller all around than the measure of the inside bottom of the tray. This will allow space for the overlap of material. Smooth the fabric down so that there are no wrinkles. Overlap the edges of the fabric and turn it so that the excess is folded onto the back of the paper. Iron the excess flap down on the back of the paper to make a smooth finish. Turn the fabric covered paper right side up and place it in the bottom of the tray. Arrange the dried flowers on top of the fabric and place the glass on top.

There are other ways to design a tray. You might consider covering the entire tray with fabric or beautiful wrapping paper. To protect this, finish with a Scotchgard fabric spray or a coating of spray varnish for paper.

Bayberry Candles in a Nutshell

Bayberry candles by Michael Butler and Danielle Frommer.

Before giving you the details about an exciting crafting experience I want to talk about berries. Specifically bayberries. For years I walked right by a very ordinary, downright scraggly bush in my yard without giving it so much as a glance. There was absolutely nothing that made me take notice of it. Not long ago I found myself standing next to it while talking to a friend. I began to pick at the bush quite absent-mindedly. I looked down at what I was picking; puny little grayish blue berries that I had not seen on that bush before. All of a sudden it had character. I began to look at other bushes that had these same tiny, seemingly insignificant berries growing all over them. I had certainly heard of bayberries, but thought of them as merely the scent that was added to candles to give them a sweet smell. I was in for a grand surprise.

The bayberry is a small shrub native to North America and found in sandy areas along the Atlantic coast from Maryland northward. It is sometimes called candleberry and wax myrtle. Bayberry candles are made from the waxy fruit of the shrub.

Michael and Danielle gathering bayberries outside of their home.

These candles are highly prized as they are practically dripless, their wax being almost entirely consumed by the flame, and the flame is said to be brighter than any other.

There is no greater treat than to drive along a beach road that is laden on both sides with wild rose bushes, beach plums growing in profusion, honeysuckle filling the air with perfume and then turn a bend, and as far as you can see, bayberry bushes! In the distance the surf and sky meet. The air is fresh and clean and the wind is blowing so that you get just a taste of salt. In the middle of all this beauty is a tiny gray-shingled cottage. In the front grow cabbages looking like enormous roses. There are planted flowers left from a summer garden.

And then we are inside. It is another world. The outside has been brought in to be enjoyed from a different perspective. The cottage has one small room with a large window. We are protected from the feel of the wind, but not the sound. The sun sparkles off the water and the waves break on the shore below. It is as though the entire ocean is performing just for us. Be-

A large box held around your neck keeps hands free for picking berries.

tween the cottage and the ocean is vegetation that is ever changing as the seasons pass. But right now, in this beautiful autumn, the scene is bayberry.

The cottage is warm and delicious with the smell of bayberries cooking on the stove. Danielle Frommer and Michael Butler are making candles.

In late summer and early fall they gather the bayberries for their delightful candles. They suggest picking the berries in the middle of October for the best yield. Since they will keep a long time there is no rush if you don't want to begin making the candles right away.

To make picking easier Danielle and Michael hang regular cardboard grocery boxes around their necks with a strip of cloth. This allows both hands to be free and avoids a lot of bending and stooping. When picking berries try to avoid mixing in lots of leaves and twigs which will have to be separated from the berries. It will take at least two full boxes to get a sufficient wax yield for a few dozen nutshell candles. In the

Berries are poured into a large pot for boiling.

winter there are not as many leaves clinging to the stems, but the berries are not very dark and are therefore not as good for candles.

Pick out as many of the leaves, twigs and other debris as possible, and then pour the berries into a large aluminum pot. How big a pot? Danielle says, "About an hour's worth of picking-time size." Next fill the pot with water so that it covers the berries by an inch or two. Bring the water to a boil and let it bubble for five or six minutes. This should then cool slowly at room temperature and is best when left to cool overnight. The wax separates from the berries and floats to the top. It is really quite marvelous how nature provides this wax. When you see the berries growing on the bushes it is hard to believe that they hold this secret.

When the wax is cool it can be lifted off the top of the water and broken into pieces. It will look as though ice has formed over the water. Sixteen to twenty ounces of wax is considered a good yield. The block of wax will still hold dirt, leaves, and twig

Boil berries for ten minutes. Skim cooled wax from surface.

pieces. These must be sifted out before making the candles.

Break the wax into pieces that will fit into a large coffee-can container. You can then throw away the remains in the pot, mostly water, berries, and leaves that have become one solid chunk.

Place the coffee can filled with wax in a pan of water and heat on the stove at a low temperature. If the coffee can is placed directly on the stove it can boil over and cause a fire. When lifting the can from the water remember that it will be very hot so use a pot holder. As the chunks of wax melt down in the can you can continue to add more chunks. When the wax is melted it will have all the debris floating in it. This must now be filtered. Michael said that they experimented with many different methods and materials, so if their way seems simple to you it is a result of much trial and error. Some of the things they tried for filtering were old jeans, gauze, and similar material. What they ended up using, because it worked the best, was the most readily available: paper towels.

Use a sharp knife. Keep your hands high when cracking open the walnuts.

Filter the hot wax through a paper towel to remove debris.

Place a piece of paper towel over the top of another empty coffee can so that it is slightly depressed into the can. Leave enough towel to hang over the edge, so that you can hold it against the outside of the can while pouring the hot wax through the filter. You have to do this a little at a time and it will take a while. Since the wax is cooling and solidifying as you work, reheat the wax in the pouring can every so often. The hotter the wax, the quicker it will sift through the towel. Do not try to eliminate the sifting by skimming the debris off the surface of the wax as it melts. This is very messy and not as effective. By the way, the wax-saturated paper towel is terrific for kindling. Throw it in the fireplace (if you have one) when you are finished with candlemaking, and it will enhance the color of your fire as well.

Once you have a can of clean wax you can begin to make candles. These can be made by using a candle mold that can be purchased in candle shops or craft stores. Michael and Danielle have an old one that they found, which resembles the original

A bent wick is placed into each nutshell before filling with wax.

ones used for tapered candles long ago. But tapered candles are not what they usually make these days. They have created a candle of their own,—a floating water candle in a nutshell. These little walnut boats can be placed in a bowl of water surrounded by flowers or berries and will glow for over an hour. Now who could resist using or giving these on any occasion?

"I'll bet you two eat a lot of walnuts," I said. "I'm just about ready for a walnut recipe book," Danielle replied. "After you eat them and make walnut bread a few times you start to think about something more creative to do with walnuts."

Michael was thinking about more practical things. "They aren't easy to open without cracking them, but I think I've figured out the quickest way." You will need a small, solid piece of wood and a sharp knife. Place the blade into the opening at the point of the walnut. Hold the nut with one hand keeping your fingers high on either side. Bare down with the other hand on the knife handle. If the shell cracks, it cannot be used. Remove the meat so that the inside is clean. If you open two or three

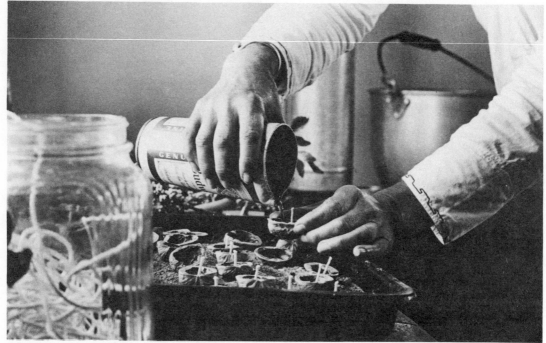

The walnuts are placed on a bed of sand for easy filling.

dozen at a time you will be able to make all candles at one time.

Filling the shells: Since the shell containers for the wax are so tiny it is difficult to fill them by holding each one. The wax may spill onto your hand, and it takes a very long time this way. After trying it this way Danielle and Michael devised a better method that works well. Fill a baking pan with sand and place the shells on the sand. Once filled with wax you can leave them to cool without fear of having them topple over before they have solidified.

Take a long wick and dip it into the hot wax. Candlewick can be found in hardware or craft stores. Stretch it out to dry. When it is dry, which will take only minutes, cut it into 1 ¼-inch pieces. Bend one third of each wick sharply and dip this bent end into fairly cool wax. The cool wax will be like gelatin and acts as the glue to hold the wick in the nutshell. Place the waxed part of the wick so that it lays in the center of the bottom of the shell. Press it down so that it will hold in place. This will dry almost immediately and the other end will be standing straight

up out of the shell. Once the wicks are all "glued" into the shells, the cooled wax can again be reheated in a pan of water on the stove.

Danielle finds that a slightly bent soda can works best for pouring. The coffee can is too cumbersome for this. Pour a little bit of wax from the stove into the smaller can so that it will always be hot. The wax is constantly cooling when exposed to the air and must be kept hot for easy and smooth pouring. When filling the walnut shells they advise not to fill them to the top right away. If the shell is filled at once to the top, there will be air bubbles on the surface. Fill each shell half way. Let this cool and then fill each to the top. The color of the candles will be green. As they burn the wax will be consumed, but nonetheless, these tiny candles should be used in water as they can cause a fire if they topple over onto a tablecloth.

When floating in a bed of flowers—whether you have used one or a dozen candles—the flame is brighter than almost any candle I have ever seen. And as if making such beautiful candles weren't enough, Michael makes tiny reed baskets as containers for them. Each little basket holds a walnut-shell candle and a tiny sprig of bayberry. A card is also inserted, telling the story of the bayberry candle and how it is made.

If you make this for gift giving, you might include a card that tells how the candles are made. It makes them so much more appreciated.

If bayberry bushes don't grow in your area, you can buy bayberry candles and melt them down for this project. I don't recommend using regular candle wax as it will burn too quickly for these small containers.

Honeysuckle Basket

Honeysuckle basket.

Mara Cary made this basic basket to demonstrate the weave that we used.

The sun was shining brightly making the silver-gray shingles sparkle. We sat on the porch, the sun on our backs, making baskets.

Mara Cary is a friend of mine who is a basket weaver, teacher, and author as well as a talented actress. Despite a busy schedule including the writing of her second book, she took a day to share her craft by teaching me how to make a simple basket. Mara has created many beautiful and unusual baskets using various materials, and she thought that the honeysuckle would be the most fun for me to start with. As it was my first lesson, I never thought that I would actually complete a basket. Mara has had a lot of experience teaching others and had, I must admit, more confidence in me than I had.

"Have you got your hiking boots on?" asked Mara's husband, Dick, as he whisked through the kitchen carrying a piece of lumber. It wasn't the last we would see of him that day. Hiking

Get your foot under a vine and pull it up with your hands.

boots for basketmaking? As it turned out, making the basket is just part of the whole experience. Of course you can buy your supplies in a craft shop, but almost everyone has access to some natural materials that can be used for basketmaking, and collecting it is half the fun.

We began walking and talking. Suddenly we were at the end of the driveway and heading down the dirt road. Turning onto a path we came to an area that held just what we needed, honeysuckle vines. "This is private property, but I have permission." Mara assured me, which was a reminder for when I was on my own. Don't go tromping after some honeysuckle only to find that you are pulling up someone else's vines. It was early fall and the best time to gather honeysuckle since it was no longer the growing season. The only tool you will need for gathering the vines is an electrician's side cutters. If you don't

Make a coil of the vines and put them in a pot to boil.

have this very handy tool, kitchen shears will do. The honeysuckle vines often grow along the ground and these nice long skinny runners are just what you will need for weaving. Just stick your foot underneath to lift one up and then get hold of it and pull. Some of the vines seem to go on forever. Gather approximately twenty of these long vines. They should be as long as a measure from your nose to the end of your arm. As we pulled at our vines Mara commented, "They seem to be growing helter skelter as though they are weaving a natural basket to hold the earth down."

When we had gathered enough we coiled them together into a wreath then wrapped the ends around three or four times to hold the coil together. You might make a loop for easy carrying. Since the honeysuckle will later be boiled in a large pot, the coil should be made into a size that will fit into your pot.

While walking home we talked about the crafting experience. Mara explained her appreciation of the evolution of basketry. "You know, this is the oldest craft practiced by man, and to this day the technique is essentially unchanged. It makes me feel good when weaving a basket to know that I am carrying on this craft just as our forebears did."

Once back in Mara's kitchen, baskets hanging everywhere, we began the basketmaking process. The honeysuckle coil is placed in a large pot just as it is, leaves and all. The pot is filled almost to the top with water and brought to a boil. The purpose of boiling the vines is to loosen the bark and preserve the vines. If you simply use the honeysuckle without first boiling it, it will be hard to remove the bark and the basket will not last as long. However, it is possible to make your basket from the fresh vines. It will not be as utilitarian because the juices that are in the vines will dry out and the vines will begin to shrink, causing the basket to become wiggly.

The recommended cooking time is from three to four hours if you would like all the bark to come off. This will create a nice smooth basket. We preferred to leave part of the bark on for a more rustic look, therefore only boiled the vines for one hour. During the cooking the room will fill with the sweet smell of honeysuckle. The water in the pot will turn a lovely pale yellow and can later be used for dyeing if you like. If not, pour it off when the boiling time is finished, and refill the pot with cold water so that you can handle the vines. Rinse them off and carry the vines outside. The next step, as you may have gathered, is quite messy.

Open the coil of vines and lay them out. We hung ours from the door handle. Wearing gloves run your hand down the vine to remove the leaves and bark. Work with the vines while they are wet. This makes removal quite easy. There we were shedding leaves and bark all over the fresh lawn and newly built porch when Dick pulled up in a borrowed truck loaded with more lumber and various other oddments. "I'm starving," he announced as he raced past us into the kitchen. The basketmaking went on.

If you are not planning to make the basket right away, the vines can be prepared for later use. Once they have been striped, wind them back into a coil. Let them dry thoroughly and store them until you are ready to make a basket. Then soak them for a few minutes in warm water. It is not necessary for all the bark to be removed. Some bark, I feel, makes the basket more interesting. In the middle of winter it is lovely to sit by the fireplace and make a basket. The excess debris can be swept right into the fire.

Back in the warmth of the kitchen we hurried Dick through his lunch so that we could reclaim the big round table. And this is where I had to muster up all my powers of concentration. While basketmaking might seem like a rather primitive craft that has a charming uninhibited quality, there is a fine line between charm and crudeness. I was a bit apprehensive about my basket leaning toward the crude side.

How to make a basket: Begin with eight long vines, all approximately the same length. These will be the stakes. Select one super long, heavier vine to be the weaver. Pinch your weaver a little off center. This means to bend or crimp it slightly with your fingernail or scissor handle. Set this aside.

Separate the stakes into four pairs. Cross two pairs, then add the other two pairs forming another cross. Use one hand to hold these stakes at the center crossing point.

Take the weaver and at the pinch point loop it aroud one side of the top pair of stakes. You will be twining or weaving with two weavers. Each time one weaver will go over the stakes, the other will go under. For each stroke, take the weaver that is farther behind and bring it forward, crossing on top of the other weaver so that they alternate.

If you hear splitting sounds when bending the weavers, it is not the vines breaking, but merely the bark that is left on the vine. The boiling has made the vine pliable.

When your weaver runs out simply insert the end into the weave. Take a new weaver, lay it into the weave right next to the old weaver and continue. As I write this I find that the basketry language is really quite fascinating.

If you keep this simple basket hand-size, it will be easier to manage. After about five times around with the weavers you can start to weave up, creating the sides. Push the stakes together and up as you weave. Keep the weavers as tight as possible. Mara says that she often works standing up so that she can

Begin your basket by crossing four pairs of stakes.

Take your weaver under and over the stakes as you work around the basket.

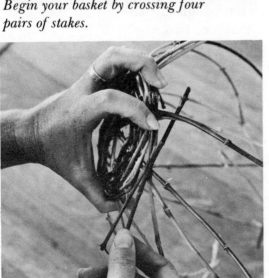

Hold the basket in one hand and try to shape as you go along.

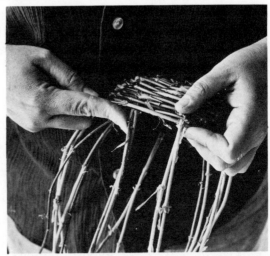

Press the weave down so that you will have a tight basket.

hold the basket against her while weaving. In that way basket-making becomes a body craft.

At this point, while I seemed all thumbs I must admit to a feeling of excitement at having created anything that was actually holding its own. The different natural colors of the honeysuckle vine and the partial bark that was darker in color seemed so exquisite. It was hard to look at this meager beginning of a basket with any kind of objectiveness. I was thrilled that it actually resembled a basket.

When the sides are the height you desire clip off the weaver end with the cutters. Cut this on the diagonal in order to create a point which facilitates poking it into the weave to secure it.

To finish, turn each pair of stakes and hold against the bottom of the basket. Clip off the excess. Now take each stake individually and loop it past one stake and push it through the basket weave along side the next stake. You may need to use a sharp implement like a knitting needle to push a space through. Pull the stake down from the bottom of the basket until the loop at the top is the desired size. Clip off the excess pieces that will be poking through the bottom and tuck the ends back into the weave.

And there you have a simple little basket. I wish I could say that now I can make all kinds of fancy baskets the way Mara Cary does, but it isn't so. I am, however, more of an appreciator. Once you have learned the technique you may want to continue. There is so much excitement to discover in the use of natural materials woven into your baskets. Mara has used seaweed and beach grasses. She has used grapevine for handles and made all sorts of shapes for as many different uses. In her book, *Basic Baskets*, she even has a basket large enough to hold her young son, Donick. "I'm right in the middle of a baby basket for my next book," she said as we were getting ready to leave. Can you imagine the thrill of carrying a baby in a basket you made?

As we left Dick's truck came bumping down the driveway. His energy seemed to collide head-on with the contrasting peaceful calm that comes over you during the basketcrafting experience. It was a nice awareness.

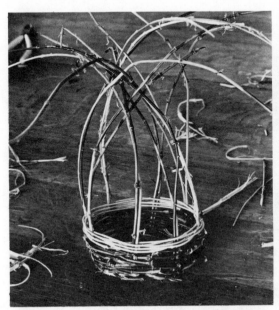
When your basket is the desired height you are ready to finish it off.

Turn the stake down on the outside of the basket to measure the border piece.

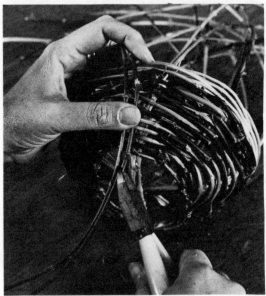
Clip off the excess stake.

Turn the stake and bring it past one set of stakes. Poke it through the weave right beside the next set of stakes.

Burr basket.

Burr Basket

While Mara and I were pursuing the honeysuckle vines, Jon Aron put down his camera to pull off the burrs that were sticking to his sweater. Burrs are seed pods. There are different kinds of burrs in different areas. Our burrs on Nantucket are from common burdock. Everytime Jon removed a burr it would then stick to his fingers, and when he turned around, more burrs had attached themselves for a free piggy back ride. In such a case it makes sense to stick the burrs to one another. If you keep doing this you will be able to create a burr basket, handle and all. It is not too practical for carrying, but when filled with dried flowers and placed on a table or sunny window sill, a burr basket can be quite unique.

If you want to make a wooly basket, there is wooly burdock. And for a great basket there is great burdock. For sea lovers there is the sea burdock. Look in a guide book for the burr that is most common in your area. Burr baskets are lots of fun. If you go walking in a field you'll be sure to find some of these thorny characters hanging around.

A burr basket can be made in minutes.

Natural Weaving

The farmhouse is surrounded by fields and woods and beyond, a couple of barns. Before entering the house the nature craft explosion begins. A stone mosaic on the front entrance is just a taste of what will follow. Rachael Love Mitchell opens the door, "Come in, come in," as though we are old friends. But we have just met.

In the hallway is a loom. Beyond, in the living room and studio, is evidence of craftwork everywhere. One would have to be here for weeks to take in all there is to see. On the couch are balls of twine and thread and fabric for soft sculpture pillows. Baskets holding milkweed pods and dried cardomom sit on the floor. Plants are thriving everywhere. The walls are simply background support for all kinds of delights. First a shell collage catches your eye, but before you can study it you are dis-

Rachael Mitchell at work in her Connecticut farmhouse.

tracted by the woven grass hanging. "I call that one 'Tribal Condominium'," Rachael says coming in from another room. She keeps bringing out new surprises as though she had a never-ending supply. "These are my garlic nests." She pulls several little baskets from a paper bag. Each one is made from the variety of trees, bushes and vines around her home. Turning back to another wall we find hard-edge assemblages, fiber collages, macramé, even sculpture. Jon remarks that Rachael is a one-person craft fair.

Right now she is in the middle of making a woven box. It is made from the weeping willow and cattails she uses in many of her projects. Rachael sits at a long low counter top between the studio and the rest of the house. On the large window sills huge home-grown gourds are drying. Eventually they will be cleaned

Natural materials such as willow and cattails are being woven together to create a box.

out and added to the many birdhouses outside the window.

To make a box, any small cardboard carton can be used for the pattern. Open it up so that it lies flat. You will do the weaving on top of this in order to follow the lines. Weeping willow branches are used for the spokes on which to weave. Dried cattails are twined with milkweed alternating with cornhusks to make an interesting pattern. This is a simple woven piece that can be done with any natural materials you might find. If you use swamp grasses, they must first be hung in a warm dark place to dry out thoroughly. For some material Rachael finds that it is easiest to weave these into the pattern using a heavy tapestry needle. Indent the weave at the corners where the flaps will fold up to create the top and sides. You will later splice and clip away the excess willow spokes. At either end leave enough

"Garlic Nests" by Rachael Mitchell.

extra spokes to insert into the weave for finishing off.

When you are ready to fold the flat weave into a box, place a wet towel under and another over the material. Leave this overnight. This will soften it so that it can be scored and folded.

Admittedly, Rachael says that she isn't sure that this will work out, but like many creative people, she is always experimenting. So, at the moment, this idea for a grass box is merely a suggestion. However, when making woven pieces from natural materials there is no formal way to do it. The materials often dictate their uses and designs. This random, sometimes unorthodox method of crafting usually produces that very quality that we are so attracted to and that makes a handcrafted piece so unique. This is especially true with crafts using natural materials. The very nature of the craft should eliminate any inhibitions you may have about trying to make something.

Woven weeping willow basket by Rachael Mitchell.

Later Rachael brought out some miniature wreaths that had been made from swamp grass. The blades of grass are braided and tied with a sprig of myrtle leaves. To preserve the leaves, dip them first in glycerin, which is a chemical preservative available in the drugstore. For a Christmas decoration holly responds quite well to this method of preservation.

For the "Tribal Condominium" and segments of another wall hanging (looking like a large canoe) cattails and woodbine are woven in and out, and the ends are tied together with heavy twine. If the material gets too dry and brittle while working it can be soaked in warm water for easy handling. This woven project doesn't take long to make and is good to use as a sampler. When first used the reed was golden yellow, but when ex-

"Tribal Condominium" by Rachael Mitchell.

posed to light it turned to a more natural color. The cattails have also turned from green to neutral. So a woven project made of natural material is a piece of art that changes its colors, adding yet another dimension to the enjoyment.

When we were almost finished learning a little bit about cattail twining, wrapping, and braiding Henry Mitchell, Rachael's husband, called us in for lunch. And while we ate delicious melted cheese sandwiches we learned all about corn-broom making from Henry. But that is another story for another book. In the meantime, if anyone knows how to make radish soup, Henry Mitchell grows big beautiful radishes and would love to have a soup recipe for them.

The reed for this woven piece in progress was golden in color, but when exposed to the light turned a natural color. Rachael Mitchell.

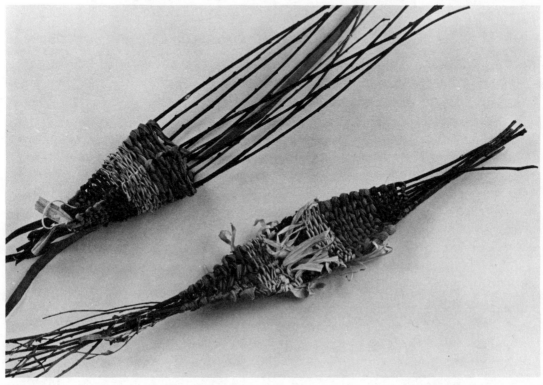

Woven Wall Hanging

Beth Trudeau makes woven hangings for her window frames. Using regular carpet twine from a weaving supplier, she weaves natural materials into the design. "I like to use the door in the studio for my frame because Louie can hang onto the thread while I work." Louie is Beth's bird and he is quite content to play with the thread, his favorite landing place.

Choose the color you want to use and begin by taping the twine at one edge of the top of a door. Pull the string down the front of the door, under the door and up the back so that it loops over the top again. Continue to wind the thread around the door until it is the desired width. Cut and anchor the string to the top of the door. You can figure approximately twelve strings, or warps, per inch.

Beth Trudeau is creating a wall hanging with yarn and found materials.

Beth does not bother with fancy equipment even though she has all the latest weaving catalogues and magazines in her studio. This is the simplest form of weaving and can be done with your hands and yarn alone. To weave, take your decorative yarn, or "weft" thread, and feed it under and over the warp threads, alternating as you go. Since this is free weaving, there is no need to restrict yourself to this procedure. The type of yarn and other decorative elements you include will influence how closely you want to follow the alternating under-and-over-pattern of weaving. A comb is Beth's basic tool for pushing the yarn around until it looks just right. Some people use a fork or similar implement. When you come to the end of a weft thread that you have been weaving back and forth, make a light knot on the last two strings of the warp.

Beth often uses heavy thick rope from the hardware store for a decorative weave. She unwinds the rope and separates it,

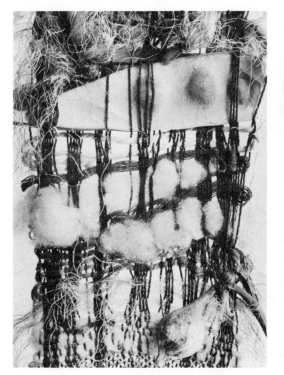

Section of woven hanging by Beth Trudeau.

causing it to look shaggy. Sometimes she dyes the rope. She
sometimes wraps the shredded rope around a piece of raw wool
and weaves that into the warp. Pull some of the wool forward
and play with it a bit until it looks the way you like it. There is
no special way to do this. It is a totally free-design concept. Beth
has many different bits and pieces of material hanging on her
wall. For the weaving elements she uses whatever suits her
mood. Milkweed pods, shells, grasses, berries, fungi, and fur,
are some of her favorites. She also uses fleece and while most
people do not have access to sheep farms at sheering time,
spinners fleece is available for about $2.00 a pound through the
mail order catalogues. Beth weaves two runners, one on the
front of the door, another on the inside. These will be used as
decorations for the sides of a window frame. Once finished and
woven to the desired length Beth cuts the strings at the top and
bottom of the door. This creates fringed borders.

Daisy or Honeysuckle Delight

While this is not exactly a craft project, it is fun, can be made on the spot, and only takes a few minutes. I thought you might like the suggestion. Children also like this for all the same reasons. You can decorate a bride, wear it around your neck, jazz up a bike parade, even your dog can get in the act.

Pick a bunch of daisies. You will need about twenty. Hold one daisy so that it is horizontal. Place another daisy behind the stem so that it is vertical. Bend the stem of the second daisy up in front of the stem of the first. Wrap the stem around its own blossom and lay this stem right next to the first stem. Place another daisy vertically behind these two stems and bend it up and hook it around its own blossom. Now you have three stems lying next to one another. Keep adding more and more daisies until the chain fits around your head, neck, or bicycle spokes. Take the first stem and wrap it around the last stem. Take a few more daisies and wrap the stems around the overlapping end stems. Tuck all stems into the others. This will obviously not last forever, but it is fun to wear for the moment. If you have made it for your bicycle spokes, simply wind the chain of daisies in and out of the spokes until the ends meet.

If you have some buttercups or clover, you can tuck them in here and there between the daisies on the wreath.

For the honeysuckle I simply split the stems with my fingernail and placed the next stem through it. It was not as delicate as the daisy wreath, but it created a sweet-smelling delight. You can do the same thing with Queen Anne's lace, which is a lot more fragile than daisies, or dandilions or even leaves. The leaves can be pinned together with their own stems.

A photogram is a picture made on photographic paper without the use of a camera. Photograms, or shadowgrams as they are also called, are easy to do and can be done by children as well as adults. Children should be supervised.

Although the basic techniques of making photograms are easily learned, some photographers and artists have used the technique to create highly ,artistic prints. Photograms are a natural medium for people who like to experiment.

One such person is Carl Moreus, a professional photographer, who is an expert on special photographic effects. However, the photograms that Carl did for us are excellent examples of the professional results you can achieve without special training or equipment.

Milkweed Photogram

Materials needed:
Photographic enlarging paper, 8"
*   × 10" (such as Kodabromide #3*
*   single-weight glossy)*
Red light bulb

Paper developer
Stop bath (acetic acid)
Fixative (hypo)
3 non-metallic trays 11" × 14"
Flashlight

All of these materials are readily available in camera stores and are the basic ingredients for all photo processing. If you are a novice, keep in mind that the people in camera stores are often photographers themselves and can probably help you. Assuming that you don't have a photographic dark room, work at night and use a bathroom with a towel under the door to keep out ambient light.

Screw in the red bulb. This is your safe light. It enables you to see what you are doing in the dark without ruining the photo paper.

Prepare your chemicals in the trays according to directions on the packages. Set the trays next to one another in this order: 1. developer, 2. stop bath, 3. hypo.

Place one sheet of printing paper on a flat surface with the shiny side up. (Be sure that the red light is the only light on and that the package of unused paper is tightly closed.) Place the

"Milkweed" photogram by Carl Moreus

milkweed pod and seeds on the paper in a design that you like. Hold the flashlight with the front lens removed about 3 feet over the paper and turn it on for about one second.

Remove the paper and place it in the developer for approximately 15 seconds. You will get the feel of developing after doing it a couple of times. If the picture comes out too black, you will have to do it again reducing the time the flashlight is on. If it is too light, leave the light on a little longer.

Take the picture out of the developer and put it immediately in the stop-bath for approximately 10 seconds. This stops the development. After the stop-bath, place the paper in the hypo for 10 minutes to fix the image permanently. At this point you can turn on the lights.

Wash the print in a tray of water by letting tap water run over it continuously for about 15 minutes. Hang the print with a clothespin to a string or hanger so that it can dry. Leave it overnight. When dry, place the print under some books to keep it flat until you are ready to mount or frame it.

Once you have found the exact time exposure, you can make all your photograms based on this amount of light time.

Pine Branch Photogram

"Pine Branches" photogram by Carl Moreus

This photogram takes the process one step further. Using the basic photogram technique, expose the pine branch on the paper. Then move the pine branch to a slightly different position on the paper and expose it again. Process and dry the print. You should have a picture that is a combination of white and gray pine branches on a black background. You can use this as a final print or: Use the first print as a "paper negative" by placing it face down on a fresh piece of paper and expose it again. This time keep the light on longer in order to penetrate the paper negative. Experiment to determine the time exposure that works best.

Process and dry the new piece of paper. The final print should be gray and black pine branches on a white background.

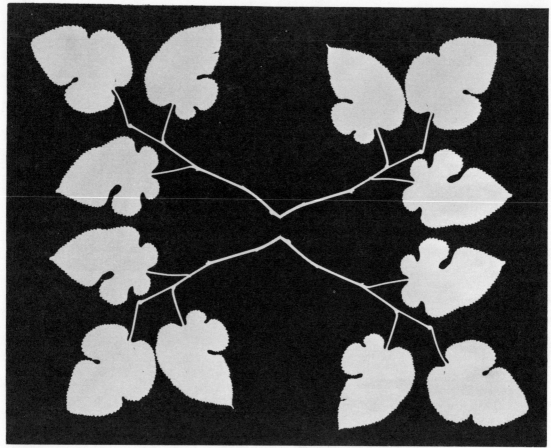

Repeat image photogram by Carl Moreus

Symmetrical Design

This was made from one sprig of leaves printed four times.

There are various ways to achieve this effect. A simple method is to make four separate photograms of leaves. Make two photograms the same way, then turn the leaves over and make two more photograms.

Paste the four photograms on heavy paper in the desired positions. You will cut the paper to get stems to butt together. When glued down, cover white edges of paper with black ink.

If you want a very neat, finished print, the pasted up photograms can be photostated. Photostat services are listed in the Yellow Pages. Ask for a PMT print.

The print can be framed as is or you can color it. This is done with water color dyes. Art stores have these dyes such as Pelikan or Dr. Martin's brand. They come in a variety of intense colors. Dilute the dye by putting a little water in a dish and add drops of dye until you achieve the color you want. Tape the print down with masking tape while coloring so that it won't curl. Using a dab of cotton, apply the dye to the print in even strokes. Cover the entire print, the dye won't affect the black part.

Maple Photogram

A print can be made showing the details of a leaf skeleton. This can be achieved by giving the paper a longer light exposure. The light will begin to penetrate the leafy parts, but not the skeleton. The results will be identical to a photograph. This composition was colored with dyes. Various colored dyes were used to get a semirealistic quality. (color plate 16)

Copygrams

Photograms can only reflect shapes and patterns. A copy machine like those used in offices or libraries reproduces the picture itself. A simple project can be done by using 8 ½″ x 11″ typing paper as a background. Place the objects such as pressed flowers, on the paper and fix them in position with a drop of rubber cement. This will hold them in place temporarily. (After using pressed flowers for photograms or copygrams you can still use them for other craft projects.) When your design is in place set it in the copier as you would with anything else you might be copying. You may have to experiment by making a few copies so that you can adjust the darkness.

In the Garden

One way to have natural materials near at hand is to grow your own. There is something special about planting a seed only to have it push through the earth to emerge as something else. Gardens are no longer limited to the back yard or farm. Window-sill planters and gardening under lights is evident in many city apartments. There is a wealth of craft projects to be explored using dried gourds, autumn chrysanthemums, rose petals, dried peppers, and, especially, herbs. Wreaths and Christmas ornaments are only a few of the projects from the garden.

A small herb patch can make life happier for the cook or craftworker. After a season of enjoying fresh herbs and flowers, they can be preserved by drying them to extend the enjoyment throughout the year.

Those wonderfully, silly-looking colorful gourds are easily grown in the garden, but are also available in the supermarket and at farmer's stands in early autumn. When dried and cleaned out they can be used as birdhouses and are fun as musical instruments for children. The seeds rattle around inside making a playful tune.

Seeds come in many colors—white, tan, brown, green, black, and gray—and are themselves wonderful to use in craft projects—perhaps a natural mosaic. Some seeds are quite interesting in shape such as the daisy-petal seeds of pumpkin and cantaloupe. Sunflower seeds are black-and-white striped, and Indian corn provides tiny red bead-like seeds. Gourd seeds are orange, creamy white, and yellow. Most seeds will retain their color even when dry, thus enabling the craftworker to explore a variety of ideas. Seed jewelry can be interesting, and one of the most unusual necklaces I have seen was made from dried red peppers and lima beans.

If conditions prevent you from gardening, keep in mind that cultivated plants are the easiest to buy. Almost all cultivated flowers, fruits, nuts, and vegetables can be found at farmer's stands, florist shops, and supermarkets.

Drying Herbs and Flowers

Drying flowers and herbs is so easy that it is hard to believe the great results that can be achieved. Most flowers will retain their original color, if not fragrance, after they are preserved. But when you dry herbs, the flavor and fragrance can be preserved for use in the winter.

Cut flowers at the height of maturity. The light-colored flowers will retain their color best. The darker flowers, especially red ones, seem to fade. Pick flowers at noon on a hot, dry day. The morning dew will have dried and there should be no trace of moisture. Flowers should be processed immediately after picking before they have a chance to wilt. If they have begun to droop, place the stems in water and wait for them to freshen up.

There are two methods of drying flowers. Some can be dried more successfully one way than the other. The method depends on the flower.

Air-drying Flowers

After picking the flowers strip off all foliage from the stems. Turn the flowers upside down and tie the stems together in small bunches. Hang them in a warm dark room that is dry.

Large pulpy flowers can be hung separately. In colonial days there were always bunches of different harvested flowers hanging from the beams by the fireplace. If you have an area in your kitchen or living room that is not too bright, the hanging flowers add to the room decoration. They really look lovely while in the process of drying. However, an attic is usually considered the best place because it is dark and dry. The bunches can be hung from a wire hanger. Be sure that the different types of flowers do not touch one another.

Allow the flowers to dry for two or three weeks. All flowers will not dry at the same rate. Those with the most moisture, will take the longest. Once the flowers are dry it is best to preserve them by spraying with a clear matte varnish. This will prevent any moisture in the air from making them limp again. Strawflowers, statice, and golden rod are some examples of flowers that air dry well.

Drying Flowers Chemically

Some flowers are preserved better in a drying agent. This method is quicker than air drying and thus preserves the color of delicate flowers that might otherwise fade. Long ago flowers were dried by placing them in a bed of sand. It was cheap, but the sand was a bit too heavy for the delicate flower and often crushed the bloom. Cornmeal and borax have also been used, but the chemical silica gel is preferred because it achieves the best results and is easy to work with.

Silica gel is a chemical for drying flowers and is sold in craft and flower shops. It is highly absorbant, light in weight, and can be used over and over again.

Pour the silica gel into a shoe box or plastic container. The box should be filled with about 1 inch of the chemical. Cut the stems of the flowers to be dried so that only short stubs remain. Stand the flowers stem down in the silica gel. If you are drying fat, heavy flowers, such as roses, tulips, or tiger lilies, place them head first on the gel. In either case, slowly sprinkle the silica gel all around the flowers until they are completely covered with the powdery substance. Dry as many flowers as you have room for. They should not touch. Cover the container and seal it so that no moisture can get in. After three days, check the flowers to see if they are ready. They will feel crisp when dry.

Remove the flowers from the silica gel and blow away the clinging material that is left on the blossom. Use wire stems to replace those that were cut off before drying. These florist wires are available in florist and hobby shops.

Once the flowers are dry protect them from reabsorbing moisture by spraying them with clear varnish or hair spray. If they are not to be used right away, store them in a dark dry area. Remember that direct sunlight will cause the color to fade. Daisies, buttercups, pansies, roses, and dogwood are some of the flowers that dry successfully in silica gel.

Drying Herbs

Herbs are soft, juicy, seed plants that were used medicinally in ancient times. They are used in cooking to impart aroma, flavor, and sometimes color. They are also used for dyeing fabrics.

Throughout history there have been innumerable legends surrounding herbs. Sesame was made famous by *Ali Baba and The Forty Thieves* and is a symbol of immortality. The Indians believed that basil brought forth feelings of sympathy and often wore a sprig when courting. The Greeks and Romans wore garlands of parsley, believing that it would keep them from becoming drunk. The ancients believed that aromatic herbs were most potent when picked under their respective planets.

In early American homes it was not uncommon to find bunches of herbs hanging from the kitchen rafters to be dried by the heat of the fire. They might have been ornamental, but they also must have collected dust and insects and not been too appealing. Today, the drying of herbs is done in several ways. For crafting—not eating—they are still hung in dry, dark places for about a week. The leaves should be crackly dry before using. Prolonged drying will cause the loss of fragrance. Remove them as soon as they are dry.

The preferred drying method is to spread the leaves on a drying rack such as the inside of a broiler pan or a cake rack. Cover them with a piece of netting or cheesecloth and set them in a dry area. There should be air circulation surrounding the rack. Shake them a bit each day so that all leaves are exposed to the air. After two or three days the herbs should be dry and ready to use.

For use in cooking, rub them between the palms of your hands so that they become powdery. Store them in air-tight containers. Don't forget labels so that you know what you've got. The leaves that are to be used in tea should be left whole. If you are planning to dry lots and lots of herbs, you should know that after two or three years, they will lose their potency. So share. Herb presents are so nice to receive.

I recently discovered an old-fashioned method for drying parsley, dill, mint, and other leafy herbs that works well. First take the leaves off of the stems and dip them into boiling, slightly salty water. This will immediately wilt the leaves. Remove from the water with a strainer. Pat them dry with a paper towel and lay them on a broiler pan. Place them into a medium-hot oven with the door open for about ten minutes. They will be dry and crisp and ready to be crumbled. Put the powdery leaves in a salt shaker for easy use. If not used for cooking, place them in an air-tight container to combine with other herbs for a potpourri.

Herb, Flower, and Vegetable Wreaths

"Oh, how fantastic. What I need is YOU. Your talent is exactly what my house needs," exclaimed a woman upon entering the shop. "Cute, cute, cute!" squealed another woman from the doorway. "Oh, Sally, I need another bunch of lavender to complete my wreath," from a loyal customer. Nobody leaves Miss Plum's Particulars without a bag of goodies tucked under one arm. Miss Plum's Particulars is the creation of Sally Pfeifer. It is a delightfully original place crammed with exciting, unusual, and often nostalgic handcrafted gifts made with natural materials. Stepping into this old-fashioned, countrylike store one finds shelves, cupboards, nooks, and niches holding unexpected surprises. There are exquisitely delicate cornhusk dolls, a variety of containers holding potpourri, baskets of spices, contemporary and traditional wreaths of dried flowers, herbs, vegetable, even driftwood. There are pressed flowers in antique frames, baskets brimming with dried flowers, seeds and pods of exotic origin, all the fixin's for a do-it-yourself project. It is like stepping into the uncomplicated world of long ago.

Hanging from the ceiling, away from the window's light, are bunches of flowers and herbs in the process of drying. They are for arrangements as well as reminders of the decorations from an earlier age. In one corner is a work area where Sally makes the flower arrangements and wreaths that are sold before she can attach the final ribbon.

"Oh, the new baby!" a regular customer has come to pick up a special floral arrangement. On top of an old roll-top desk sits a wicker basket. A newborn baby sleeps contentedly. A month ago the desk held less important things like order slips and billing information. Now, during working hours, it is home for Sally's baby. "This is the second Miss Plum," she said, by way of introduction. Sally's sister, Susan, helps out a great deal between minding the store and helping with the children. But everyone has been waiting to see the new baby, and this morning they seem to come in as much for a look as for dried materials.

Sally has had Miss Plum's for over five years. "My mother always had an herb garden," Sally told me. "I guess flowers have always been part of my life, and I feel comfortable working with

16. *"Maple" photogram by Carl Moreus*

17. *Bayberry candles by Danielle Frommer and Michael Butler*

18. Honeysuckle chain

19. "Tribal Condominium"
by Rachael Love Mitchell

20. Burr basket

21. *Woven hanging by Beth Trudeau*

22. *Honeysuckle vine basket*

23. *Wreath by Elsie Herbert*

24. *Dried flower arrangement by Sally Pfeifer*

25. Wreath by Sally Pfeifer

26. Corn husk doll by Carol Patenaude

27. *Rose petal bead necklace*

28. *Sand cast candle*

29. Sailor's valentine
by Charles McQuire

30. African necklace by Elen Schwartz

31. "Orange Stripe" assemblage by Henry Petzel

32. "Memory Pockets" by Kathy Kelm

33. Driftwood wreath

Sally Pfeifer makes dried arrangements at Miss Plum's Particulars.

them. It's very natural for me. I never get tired of making arrangements. Each one is a new challenge. I really love to make arrangements for special occasions." Recently Sally made up the decorations for an old-fashioned wedding. The nosegays, bridal bouquet, boutonnieres, and all the centerpieces were her dried-flower creations. She used dusty rose and the natural fall colors of brown. She said that it was quite unusual and a true creative challenge.

While she is the designer of many of the bouquets and wreaths, Sally also carries the work of other fine craftworkers in the area, which lends a variety to her shop. The smell of the drying herbs, spices, and flowers adds to ones desire to make a floral wreath or other project using these materials. In between tending to the baby and waiting on customers, Sally took the time to share her wreathmaking methods with us.

Begin with a wire florist ring. This can be purchased in a florist shop or craft shop, or you can make your own. They are usually from 10 to 20 inches in diameter; one that is 10 or 12 inches is a good size to start with. Use bunches of dried Artemisia for the

Finished wreath by Sally Pfeifer.

bulk of the wreath. If you place two large bunches so that their
stem ends face each other, they will encircle the wire ring. Wire
the Artemisia to the ring with thin wire that comes on a spool.
Use fresh sprigs of Artemisia to insert here and there. If you
find that the material you are working with is too dry and therefore brittle, you can spray it with a little water while you work.
This will make it more pliable. Keep a squirt bottle filled with
water next to your work area. Into this basic wreath you can
insert a variety of dried herbs and spices to make it your own
creation. For a delicious scent, you might spice it up with lavender, cinnamon sticks, bay leaves, or rosemary. Dried tansy, cardamom, wild iris pods, and strawflowers add color. Tie small

Bunches of dried Artemisia are used for the base of the wreath.

Glue pieces of dried flowers here and there.

To insert dried materials wrap florist wire around the stems.

sticks onto pods and flowers that do not have strong stems. These sticks resemble wooden match sticks, are tied with thin wire, and will allow easy insertion into the Artemisia. Sally's

Dried vegetables, such as hot peppers, add color and interest to the wreath.

Add more Artemisia where needed to fill out the wreath.

Finish wreath by adding a decorative bow.

wreath is adorned with dried red peppers, which makes a delightfully charming and colorful holiday look.

Drying Vegetables: Hot peppers are not only red like Sally's but yellow and bright chartreuse as well. These are the long skinny ones which can be used in floral or fruit arrangements, wreaths, and even strung to wear around your neck as jewelry. I know it sounds silly to have a string of hot peppers around your neck, but they are really very unusual. Like the flowers and herbs, peppers look beautiful while drying. Thread the peppers with heavy-duty thread or florist wire so that you can easily tie the two ends together creating a circle. Hang them in a dry area such as the kitchen as a decoration while they are drying. When ready to use, spray the peppers with glossy clear varnish to preserve them.

An unusual suggestion for an arrangement is the use of dried artichokes. They can be grouped together or arranged with other vegetables. Choose very fresh artichokes and hang them in a dark dry area. Tie them from the stem and hang upside down for several weeks. To create an open rosette form, put paper between the leaves to force them open while drying.

Perhaps you thought it silly to hang red peppers around your neck, well what about combining them with garlic? Actually, once garlic bulbs are dried out they have no odor and are very interesting. Perhaps you would rather stick to using them in a dried arrangement mixed with onions and artichokes. Dried cauliflower, cabbage, broccoli, and brussel sprouts can be used beautifully alone or combined with sprigs of leaves and berries.

Finishing the Wreath: When adding spices or dried herbs to the wreath it is a good idea to put a little bit of glue on each piece before inserting it. This will secure it better than simply sticking it into the Artemisia. For the final decoration Sally uses a combination of ribbons to create a bow. She places a patterned ribbon over a contrasting velvet ribbon and makes a bow that is nice and full. This is not tied but rather secured in the center by wrapping a piece of wire around the ribbon. Leave enough of the wire so that it can be inserted into the wreath. A small piece of cardamom is glued to the center of the bow. Snip any excess wire after the entire wreath is finished.

Flower Arrangements: Later, while feeding the baby, Sally talked about flower arranging. When using dried flowers, certain ones work best. She suggests globe amaranth, cockscomb, golden yarrow, tansy, and strawflowers. These are found in herb and florist shops already dried. For a floral arrangement she suggests finding the container first. Sally keeps an eye out for unusual ones of different color, size, and shape as well as style. "Often a container indicates the sort of house the arrangement will go with," she says. "The flowers should be chosen with this in mind." For instance, an early American pitcher or cheese crock might be used for an older home. The flowers might be strawflowers, crysanthemums, or golden yarrow. A large block of styrofoam or floral clay is first placed into the container. One at a time, the stems of the dried flowers are poked into this. As the arrangement develops you have to check it to see which way to proceed. If stems are weak or need lengthening, a stiff green wire can be attached to the real stem,

Dried floral arrangment for the new baby by Elsie Herbert.

then inserted into the styrofoam. This wire is available in garden shops. Wooden toothpicks can also be used.

Begin with the large heavy flowers first. Then fill in with the lighter sprigs, such as baby's breathe, which are more delicate. The more you arrange flowers the better you will get a feel for it. Soon you will know exactly which flowers you like best when combined with others. Statice can be found in pink, yellow, white, and blue and looks well when arranged with globe amerinth. A bouquet to celebrate the arrival of a new baby should be simple and delicate combining light, pale-colored flowers.

The strawflowers that Sally uses in many of her arrangements are grown and dried by a woman in the area. "She can really grow beautiful flowers," says Sally. "The white and pale pink are very unusual and extremely difficult to get." Sally uses these delicate ones, often combined with bits of purple larkspur or lavender and wispy baby's breathe.

Sally Pfeifer with Lindsay in front of Miss Plum's Particulars.

Dried floral arrangement by Sally Pfeifer.

Potpourri from Miss Plum's Particulars.

Potpourri

The delicious smelling potpourri is another of Sally's specialties. At Christmas time potpourri of lemon verbena, rose, and geranium petals and lavender perfume the air suggesting the freshness and fragrance of a summer garden. It is so easy to make your own blend that I thought you might like a few suggestions. I find that the more I become involved with the herbs and spices, the more I want to know how to use them. Just being in Miss Plum's Particulars for an afternoon heightens ones desire for some of Sally Pfeifer's old-fashioned scents.

Roses have always been the basis of sweet-smelling mixtures. In olden days women put a layer of partially dried rose petals into a crock. These rose petals were covered with a layer of salt and another layer of rose petals alternating until the jar was full. The whole thing was allowed to cure or rot. The French verb *pourrir* means to rot, and from this came the name potpourri pronounced "pō-pō-rē". Today the method for drying flowers and herbs for potpourri is by air drying as previously described. Simply letting the roses dry in the sun with plenty of air circulation is the best way, especially in the summertime. The dried petals can then be put in a glass container. Keep this away from the light so that the color doesn't fade. Once dried, the jar should be kept air tight to keep moisture out.

Lavender leaves and blossoms have a beautiful fragrance and can be combined with the rose petals. You might add the leaves of lemon verbena, geraniums, sage, and woodruff. Dried citrus peel of lemon, lime, oranges, and grapefruit create another kind of potpourri.

In order to blend the various scents and to be sure that the fragrance lasts, you must add a fixative to the mixture. Orris root is the most popular fixative and is usually available through florists, nurseries, some drugstores, places where herbs are sold, or mail order supply houses. (See Source list)

To make your potpourri, toss all the dried leaves and buds into a large bowl. The buds are to pretty it up. Add fixatives and spices. For every cup of dried petals you should add a teaspoon of fixative and a teaspoon of spices. If you want, you can add a drop of fragrant oil to hold the aroma. A drop of your favorite perfume might be just the thing. Toss the mixture around lightly with a wooden spoon. Place this in a closed container and leave it for several weeks. From time to time if you have more dried scents, you can just toss them in also. Stir this up occasionally while it is aging.

When aged this potpourri can be placed in an apothacary jar or you might like to make sachets or room fresheners with it. Tuck a sachet into a box with an elegant lacy handkerchief for a special gift.

Herbal Beauty Aids

Herbal Bath Oil
For centuries herbs have been used in the bath for relaxing tired muscles. While there are all kinds of commercial bath oils, it is fun to make your own refreshing bath scent. Place a mixture of herbs in a small bag of cheesecloth and drop it into your bath water. The herbs will steep in your hot bath just as in making tea. The most popular herbs are mints, thyme, sage, rosemary, pennyroyal, lavender, angelica, and lemon balm or lemon verbena.

Herbal Skin Fresheners
Fill a jar with equal parts of crushed rose petals, lavender leaves, and lemon verbena or mint leaves. Pour unscented rubbing alcohol over all filling to the top of the jar. Cover the jar and let this stand for two weeks. Shake it up occasionally. Strain the liquid through cheesecloth and pour into a pretty bottle. The rose petals, elder flowers, or calendulas have astringent qualities.

Hair Rinse
If you boil rain water or softened bottled water with lemon verbena leaves or the tips of rosemary, you will have a delightfully fragrant hair rinse. Simmer this for half an hour then strain. Pour it through your hair after shampooing.

Going to a Wedding
Forget the rice. Throw dried rose petals at the bride and groom instead.

Pomander Balls

Almost everyone has made a pomander ball to sweeten a closet at one time or another. But in case you've forgotten about this lovely project here are a few reminders. Select fresh, firm fruit such as orange, lemon, lime, kumquat (for a tiny pomander), or apple. To make two pomander balls, you will need 3 ounces of whole cloves, 2 teaspoons of powdered orris root, and 1 table-spoon of ground cinnamon. Orris root is often available in the spice section of the supermarket, sometimes in a drugstore, and always at an herb store.

Using a sharp instrument, such as a skewer, make holes to insert the cloves into the skin of the fruit. Take care not to make a straight line, but rather a random pattern, so that the skin will not split. If a split occurs, it will heal in a few days.

When the fruit is completely covered with cloves place it in a bowl and sprinkle the mixture of cinnamon and orris root over the whole thing. Place the fruit in a small bag made of cheese-cloth so that air can get at it. Hang in a dry, warm place so that the fruit will shrink. As the fruit dries it will shrink and no part of the skin will show. This should take about three weeks.

Tie the pomander balls with decorative ribbon and catch with a bow at the top. A pretty cord can be attached at the top so that it can be hung in a closet. Besides smelling spicy and fresh, it will protect clothing from moths.

Jane Kasten grinding rose petals for a necklace.

Rose-petal Beads

A beaded necklace made from rose-petal paste lasts forever.

Materials needed:
Rose petals (shopping bag full)
Meat grinder
Dental floss or waxed thread
Necklace clasp
Straight pins

When Jane Kasten married Sam she wore a string of eighty-year-old rose-petal beads. Her grandmother, Dagmar Christensen, had made them when she was a young girl and the beads have grown more lovely with age, still retaining the full fragrance of roses.

Jane and Sam are craftworkers. Far from her original studies as a linguist at the University of Iowa, Jane now works as a seamstress for the Nantucket Looms. Sam is a weaver.

The Kastens live in a home that they built. It is designed with the simple elegance of the Shakers. As we sipped herb tea in the peaceful, quiet kitchen which overlooks Jane's garden she shared the rose-bead recipe.

So you can still go on enjoying the roses, it is best to select rose petals that have fallen on the ground. However, they must be fresh. There are many varieties of roses and they may all be

A grapevine basket by Mara Cary is used for gathering rose petals.

used successfully. You can usually find the pasture rose on rocky hillsides and in dry thickets during June or July. The meadow rose is found near meadow walls and along fences in June. These are usually bright crimson in color and have large red fruit or rose hips. June is the time to gather your rose petals. Jane says that to make a good-sized necklace will take about sixty beads—a child's necklace will consist of about forty. "To be sure that you have enough petals before starting, I would recommend filling a standard shopping bag," Jane suggests. They should be fresh and moist.

Years ago women would crush and beat the fresh petals with a pestle for at least two hours. The best way to prepare your petals is to put them through a meat grinder. If you don't have a meat grinder, you can first cut the petals up into tiny pieces with scissors before pounding and crushing them into a fine paste. The meat grinder will turn the rose petals into a claylike substance. After grinding, place the petals into a cast-iron skillet. The petal paste affects other metals and will turn another pot black. Put the rose petal paste through the meat grinder daily for fifteen days. Each day the petal paste will become more dense. As the rose-petal paste stays in the skillet it will begin to turn darker and darker.

Form the petal paste into beads by rolling small amounts in your hands. Make each bead twice the size you want. They will shrink as they dry. Stick a pin into each bead while it is still moist or they will dry too hard to thread. Place the pins into something soft like a cork or bulletin board so that air will circulate around the beads. It will take about a week for them to dry thoroughly. String the beads on strong linen, button thread. This is a waxed thread, or you might use dental floss. Polish each bead with a soft cloth. You can alternate a rose-petal bead with another bead such as a semiprecious stone of a different color. Jane's baby necklace has amber beads between the rose beads. Attach a clasp at the back for a finish. This is called a jewelry finding and can be found in craft stores. You might even have an old necklace from which you can remove the clasp. The beads will become harder and darker and more polished-looking with age and use.

Gourds

Gourds are old-timers in the garden. No one knows for sure where they came from, but they are usually placed in the squash family, although they are not edible. Long before pottery these funny-shaped objects that grow on vines were used as bowls, ladles, and cooking utensils. In colonial days they were used as water dippers, as cooking pots—by putting heated stones in them—and as fishing-net floats. Once dry the seeds rattle around inside and the gourd is a grand musical instrument. Even Indian snake charmers used gourds as pipes.

As with most other primitive materials the gourds' services have been replaced by manufactured items, and now they are used exclusively for decoration. These bright-colored odd-shaped characters have a compelling charm about them. They are sometimes funny-looking, beautiful, deformed, ugly, warty, and outrageous. They are always available in the fall at fruit stands and in the supermarket, but are also extremely easy to grow in a home garden.

Whether purchased or home grown, gourds have to be left to dry before anything can be done with them. Many people display them in a bowl for a month or two, then put them away in a dry warm place like a furnace room. Left alone for several months they will become completely dry and hard. Handle them carefully during the drying period. It can take as long as six months, so be patient. A forgotten gourd is a happy gourd. While they are beautiful in color and design when fresh, they turn slightly brown when completely dry.

To craft with a gourd, clean with soap and water after it is dry. Cut the gourd open and remove the seeds. These can be planted for next year's crop. Plan where you want to cut into the gourd. Perhaps you will make a birdfeeder, so you will cut a circle out of the front. To cut through the hard, dry skin you will need a pocket or kitchen knife. The inside has a soft ivory, velvet-textured surface. To remove this soak in warm soapy water and scrape it out with a spoon. The interior will feel like leather.

Drill a hole in the top and insert a wire or cord. Tie a knot to the inside and hang the other end of the cord to a tree. Fill the gourd with bird seed. If you want to decorate the gourd, it can

A gourd birdfeeder is perfect for the chickadees.

be painted and then shellacked. Most gourds that you buy are already semidry and lacquered or varnished so that the outside is shiny. A coating of wax will protect the outer skin. The gourds that I used had been sitting in a bowl for three months. I became impatient and cut into them even though I knew they weren't as dry as they should be. The inside was wet and pulpy like the inside of a pumpkin. It was easy to clean it out with a spoon. The holes in the top for the cord were made with a sharp instrument like an awl or ice pick. I think that a sharp nail would work as well. Perhaps in time the gourd will rot away, but in the meantime the birds are happily feeding from it. The chickadees in particular find this a perfect feeding station.

Spiderweb Art

Materials needed:
White spray paint
Stiff paper
Spray varnish or plastic coating
Scissors

Spiders are impressive weavers. Some webs are precise geometric forms, elegant, beautiful, and quite effective as fly catchers. Spiderweb patterns are interesting to preserve and exhibit as paintings.

Before heading for the nearest garden spider, keep in mind that spiderwebs are extremely delicate. Did you know that spiderwebs are spun of silk? In fact, spider silk is finer, lighter, and stronger than the silk that is spun by the silkworm. For centuries people have been trying to figure out how to economically harvest spider silk for commercial use. Because of its extreme fineness, spider silk is used in some optical instruments.

You may not have noticed spiderwebs near where you live because they are almost invisible. Spiders are most active in the

Look for a delicate spider web in the garden.

summer especially on sunny days. Most web collectors favor the round geometric orb webs, although spiders spin many different-shaped webs. If one is damaged, they usually have a new one woven by the next day. How co-operative!

Begin by spraying the web gently with paint. Stand about ten or twelve inches away from the web. If you are using white paint, the background paper should be black or a dark color. If you would like to use black paint, then the paper should be white or a pastel color. Construction paper is good for this project. Get a feel for how to spray the paint before applying it to the web. I know this sounds fairly elementary, but the web is a lot more delicate than you imagine. I ruined two or three before I was able to control the amount of pressure. Some people spray sideways rather than head on. Check to see which way the wind is blowing also. Since you are an uninvited guest, be sure that the spider has moved out before intruding and taking over its home. After all, the spider has done all the work. Spray the paint evenly all around the web. Keep spraying until the web is completely covered.

Spray the web with paint before transferring to paper.

Bring the paper into contact with the web from the back. Hold the paper against the web gently and spray the front with a plastic spray. I use an acrylic matte varnish because it works both as an adhesive and a protective coating. The web will stick to the paper. Spray carefully around the edges. If the web isn't completely adhered it will collapse in places. When all is secure, snip the lines around the edges with a scissors. Do not simply rip the web from the guide lines as you pull the paper forward. By using the scissors you insure a clean break exactly where you want it rather than where the line is weakest.

You can mount the spider art on a matte board and frame it or put it into a glass frame. Or you can just tack it up as is for the moment's enjoyment.

Another way to do this is on a rock. Paint or find a dark rock and attach the web to it in the same way you removed it onto the paper. Coat the surface with spray varnish to protect it. You might add a little piece of felt to the bottom to make a paper weight or a book end or simply a decoration on a table. Either way, you can appreciate the work of the first Op artist, the common garden spider.

Catch the web on construction paper and cut the web to fit.

Cornhusk Dolls

Materials needed:
Husks from 6 ears of corn
String
8-inch pipe cleaner
Black felt pen
Pan of warm water

In our colonial days little children often played with dolls made of cornhusks. Today they are appearing more and more often at craft fairs, and this is one of the many old crafts in which interest is being revived through the magazines. There is almost no material that we cannot find in craft shops or through the mail, so even if it is not corn season or you live in a large city, you can purchase the cornhusks for this project.

The exquisite dolls made by Carol Paternaude are also pictured on the color pages and show the dolls delicately dressed in their period costumes. They are sitting on small wooden benches made by Carol's husband.

Cornhusk doll by Carol Patenaude.

Directions: The cornhusk is the outer covering of an ear of corn. It takes husks from about six ears of corn to make one doll. It is best to begin by stripping the husks from the ears of corn and soaking them in a pan of warm water for about five minutes. This will make them pliable and easier to work with.

Make the head first by tearing off a ¼" wide strip from one of the husks. Rip it down the full length of the husk and roll it into a ball. Secure it by pushing a short straight pin into the ball.

Using another strip of cornhusk, roll it into a 1 ½ inch ball for the upper body. Secure this with a short, straight pin. Take 2 or 3-inch-wide strips of cornhusk and loosely wind them around the pipe cleaner to create the arms. Cut off the excess and tie the ends with string.

A full-length strip of husk that is approximately 1 inch wide is then draped over the head from front to back. Twist the pieces around just under the head and tie it tightly with a string to create a neck. There will be extra husk below the string. It can be trimmed later.

Slip the pipe-cleaner arms under the neck piece. Hold it in position and slip the upper-body ball under this strip of husk. This will hold the arms in place. Next twist the ends of the long strip of husk around in order to secure the upper-body ball. Tie with string. This will create the waist.

A skirt to cover the body can be made from the husks or you might want to sew your own costume right onto the doll. To make a skirt take a long strip of husk. Place the center of the husk on the waistline. If you use several husks, the skirt will be quite full. Tie this strip at the waist with a string. Let the top ends fall down over the string. Add as many husks as you feel is enough to make a full skirt. Once the skirt is complete, cut the hemline so that it is even.

If you are not sewing a blouse from fabric, you can make one with 2 strips of corn husk ½-inch wide. Place one strip over one shoulder and cross it in front of the doll. Do the same on the opposite side. Cross the strips in the back. Tie these strips at the waist with string. Make a 1-inch wide waistband to cover the string and secure in the back with a pin or by creating a bow with the cornhusk.

Hair for the doll can be made from thread, such as brown or yellow embroidery thread, or you can use the corn silk. Take several strands at a time and glue them to the head of the doll with white glue. Make a small ribbon bow and secure it with a pin. If you prefer a bonnet, this can be made with fabric or a strip of corn husk.

Using a black felt-tip pen you can draw a face for the doll. A simple representation is usually best. Dots for eyes and nose are fine with a small round mouth and perhaps some red coloring for the cheeks. It is not difficult and does not have to appear realistic to be effective.

Cornhusk doll by Carol Patenaude.

By the Sea

When we mention crafting projects using materials from the seashore most people think of shells. There are, of course, endless varieties of shells to be found depending on the area or type of seashore you visit. But there is much more. The plant life that grows near beaches is often surprisingly beautiful and can inspire many new ideas. Combined with materials from the fields, dune grasses can be woven quite easily into wall hangings or other less time-consuming projects.

Driftwood is another collectable and can be used in creating an assemblage or hanging mobile. Often silvery and worn smooth, these odd pieces of wood that have been deposited on the beach have become real treasures.

The best time for beachcombing is at low tide. After a storm you can usually find the most interesting deposits of stones, shells, and seaglass which the turbulence of the waves have churned up. Since the shore line is constantly changing you can visit the same area over and over again always finding something new. If you find shells that have tar on them, clean with linseed oil to restore the luster.

The greatest variety of collectables is found along tropical beaches, but every beach, even those lining fresh-water lakes, can offer the crafter something of interest.

However, you do not have to eliminate craft projects requiring a variety of beautiful and unusual shells just because you do not live near a beach. Every shell imaginable is available from shell shops and mail-order houses.

Collecting Shells

A walk on the beach has always seemed romantic. Perhaps it is a sense of freedom one feels when removed from the main stream. The clean, fresh air, the breeze blowing off the water, the awareness of the uncontrollable tides make us somehow more in touch with our feelings.

On beaches where shells collect, people pick them up, almost unconsciously. Often people will collect the shells from the beach during a walk and deposit them back in the sand at the end of the walk. For those people, the collecting experience was satisfying in itself. Beachcombing for shells is an interesting study in art appreciation. What is it we are looking for in the myriad of little shapes? Perfect symmetry, a design, a pattern? Or are we looking for the exotic, unusual, hoping to find a shark-eye moon snail, the only one on the beach?

Many beach walkers express personal fancies by picking up only one type of shell. Others seek out the sea glass that has been smoothed over by the turbulence of sand and sea. Once home, the shell collector frequently deposits the new shells in a glass container along with the shells from other beaches, collected at other times. The nice thing about shells is that it doesn't matter what you do with them, they always remind the collector of a good feeling. Many shell collectors think that there is only one way to show off the shells to the greatest advantage and that is in a beautiful glass jar. There is no argument there. They are simply beautiful as is.

Sometimes the shells and beach stones look prettiest when wet because they become dull after they have dried out. You may prefer to fill the jar with water. Shells and stones can also be coated with glossy varnish to create that underwater effect.

Shell Sampler

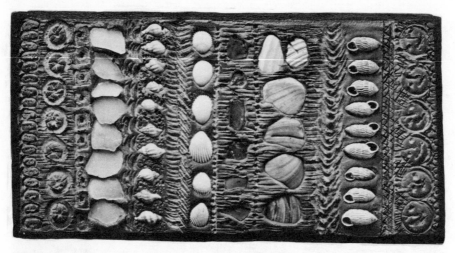

Shell relief by Rachael Mitchell.

Materials needed:
molding for a 10 × 15" frame (if
  you prefer another size frame,
  buy molding to the right size)
Piece of plywood or masonite ¼"
  thick 10 × 15"
Bag of Plaster of Paris (or can of
  modeling compound)
Picture wire for hanging
Selection of shells
Two screw eyes

Sometimes the most ordinary shells can be made into a most
unusual-looking collage. When you first look at a well-designed
display there is a sudden impulse to ask where those unusual
shells have come from. But often, upon a closer look, you discover that the common scallop shell, or even a broken piece
from a clam shell has been utilized.

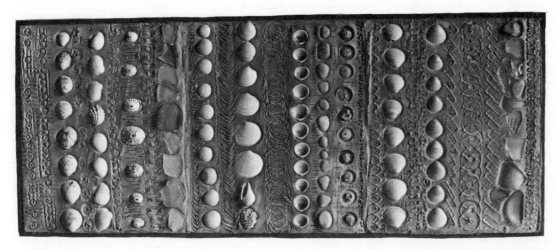

Shell relief by Rachael Mitchell.

Rachael Mitchell combines shells, sea glass, and textured backgrounds to create abstract assemblages. For this she uses a shadow box frame.

Preparation: You can make a frame using 1-inch molding. Back the frame with ¼-inch-thick plywood or masonite. Into this you put the background material that will hold your shells.

Next draw a rectangle the same size as the frame on a piece of paper. Arrange your shells on the paper in the design pattern you want.

Now fill your boxed frame with modeling compound or plaster of Paris. This is easy to do with a palette or butter knife. Fill to within ⅛-inch of the tops and smooth it out. Place the shells into the background material as you have planned them. Since plaster of Paris will harden much faster than modeling compound, for a first project it might be an advantage to use the slow-setting compound. These are both available in hardware or craft stores.

Textures and patterns can be made on the background in many ways. As the paste or plaster dries it will reach a stage that

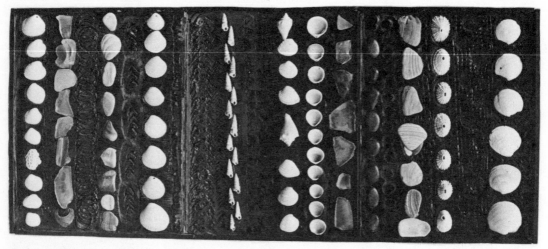

Shell relief by Rachael Mitchell.

is good for pressing objects into it in order to create interesting patterns. Some useful items are buttons, a screwdriver, screening, kitchen implements, pens, pencils, silverware, jewelry, etc. Use your imagination when developing a textured design. Once the impressions are made, remove the object. When the background is completely dry your shells will be imbedded securely and the patterns you have created will be permanent.

Rachael often uses colored backgrounds of earth tones. Burnt umber is added to the modeling compound to change the color. Sand color or similar subtle tones are other favorites. Acrylic paint can be added to the modeling compound to create the background color of your choice.

Try making a small assemblage first so that you get the feel of working with the materials. When dry it will be heavy. Use screw eyes and picture wire for hanging.

Plaster-cast Shell Assemblage

Shell relief by Rachael Mitchell.

Working with Plaster of Paris is easier than you may think. It is great as a background material for setting things into. It is also excellent for casting.

The main thing to remember when working with plaster is to be careful about measuring the amount of water in relation to the amount of plaster. The directions are on the container. Follow them, even though you may think you need more water at first.

Plaster is available in hardware stores, lumberyards, and wherever building and painting materials are sold.

To Make a Plaster Casting: To make a compartmented plaster casting you will need a sturdy box that is about 3 inches deep by whatever dimensions you would like to use as a frame. The compartments can be made by setting boxlike shapes into the plaster after it has been poured. The boxlike shapes can be wood blocks or little plastic or cardboard boxes, square bottles, etc.

Get your materials all set before pouring the plaster or you may find yourself running around looking for boxes while your

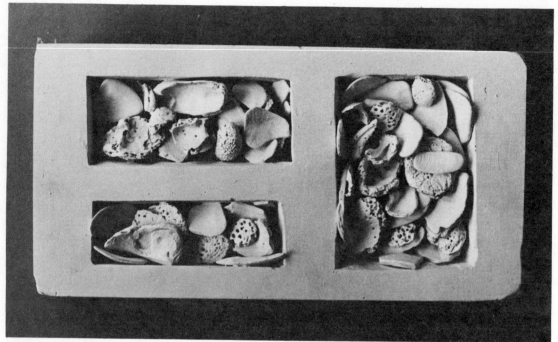

Stone-and-shell assemblage in plaster by Ann Jones.

already poured plaster is making a brick out of itself. Pour about 2½ inches of plaster into the box. Wait a bit for this to begin to set. Place your blocks in a pattern into the plaster. Set them in to a depth of about 1 or 1 ½ inches. They shouldn't be so deep that the shells will get lost in them.

When the plaster sets up hard, remove the blocks. Let the plaster mold dry overnight.

Once dry, plaster can be sanded and painted if desired. Into the compartmented mold place the desired shells. Ann Jones has used ordinary shells and pieces of bone that were found at the water's edge. Elmer's glue holds the shells in place. Once you have the assemblage designed and glued let it dry for a half hour. Ann then painted over the whole thing—shells and plaster—using white acrylic paint. If you want to add a shiny finish, coat the entire assemblage with glossy polymer medium or varnish available in craft stores and art-supply stores. This can be hung as is or mounted on a black background board.

Shell Wind Chimes

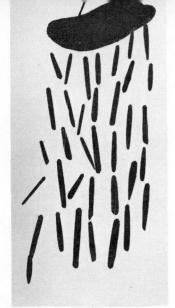

*Sea urchin wind chime
by Suzanne Bloom.*

Wind chimes made from shells are a delight to the senses. The pleasant faint tinkling sound from a doorway can be a reminder of a pleasant experience at the shore. So even though this craft project may be out of sight it is not out of mind. Each type of shell has its own sound depending on size, shape, and configuration. When a wind chime is made using only one type of shell the sound they make when coming into contact with one another is beautifully harmonious.

Sea Urchin Chime

Sea urchin spines almost look man-made. While they are not common on beaches they are readily available through craft shops and mail order outlets. This sea urchin chime hangs from a piece of driftwood. The wood is cleaned as well as possible with a wire brush. It is then stained with wood stain available in hardware or paint stores. A coating of matte varnish will give it a finished look.

An electric drill, such as a Dremel Moto-Tool, is needed to drill the holes into the sea urchin spines. A hand drill can be used but is not as effective. You may crack a few shells before perfecting this. The power drill moves at high speed which helps avoid breaking the shell.

Five spines are tied at intervals on monofilament fishing line, which is available wherever fishing equipment is sold. The lines should hang close together because the spines are long and thin. When they hit one another it is a delightful delicate sound. Drill holes in the driftwood and tie each line through the hole, knotting it at the top.

Sundial wind chime by Suzanne Bloom.

Sundial Chime

The sundial wind chime is made in the same way as the sea urchin spine chime except that there are fewer shells and fewer·
lines. The sundial shells are more massive and should be placed
farther apart. They are not as delicate as the sea urchin spines
and create an altogether different sound. Sundial shells are
particularly pretty. They have a distinct pattern that travels
around the shell in a concentric path. Sundial shells are only
found on warm-water beaches. If you are not living or visiting a
tropical beach, you will have to buy these beauties from a shell
or craft store.

163

Scallop shell wind chime by Suzanne Bloom.

Scallop Chime

Scallops are found almost everywhere. Different species are found throughout the beach areas of the United States. They vary in size and coloration. Some Japanese scallops are accommodating enough to come in various pastel colors. Since I didn't have Japanese shells, I tried my own version of coloring shells. They can be painted with acrylic paint, but I don't care for the density of color, nor do I like the shells to look as if they have been painted. In an experiment I dyed some shells as you would Easter eggs. In a glass of hot water I placed one teaspoonful of vinegar and two or three drops of food coloring. The shell was placed into the liquid for about fifteen minutes. The color that took left the shell with a faint coloring that looked quite natural. Pink and sky-blue were the nicest, I thought.

The scallop-shell chime is hung from one larger scallop shell. Special care must be taken when drilling the holes. For this chime, five holes were drilled around the bottom of the large shell and another at the top for hanging. Additional holes were drilled in the scallop shells that hang from the fishing lines.

Placing the shells is both an "eye" and "ear" decision. Different sizes make different sounds. Experiment. You may like the variety of sound made by different-size shells. If you decide to use various-size shells, arrange them so that they hit against one another as they move. The potential for designing forms and sounds together in one piece is unlimited.

A mobile is created with shells and sea-glass.

Shell and Sea-glass Mobile

Materials needed:
*Wood disk used for basket base 10
  inches in diameter*
Lightweight monofilement fishing
line or nylon thread
Shells, sea glass, stone, bones, etc
3M super strength glue
Leather thong 14 inches long

The principle of this hanging mobile is the ability of the decorative shells and glass to move up and down when you pull them. In this way, the viewer becomes a participant and can change the relationship of the pieces to one another. It can be any size and any proportion. It can also be made with anything that you collect at the beach. Once you know how to make it, the creative possibilities are endless.

I used a wooden disk that is found in craft shops for the base of a basket. The holes are drilled around the perimeter ½ inch from the edge and ½ inch apart. They are ⅛-inch holes. You can make your own disc by drilling holes in a piece of plywood.

The fishing line is threaded up through one hole and down through the one next to it, thus enabling you to pull each strand up and down. Each line is cut to 4 feet. Thus, once threaded they will produce two 2-foot lines. To the end of each line attach a sea treasure. Some shells have natural holes in them. These are best to use because you avoid the problem of drilling a hole in a hard substance. As mentioned previously, the easiest way to drill holes in shell is with a Dremel Moto-Tool. A small bit inserted into a hand drill is an alternative.

Tie the shell and glass pieces to the ends of the strands. Use 3M Super Strength glue to attach the thread to pieces of glass or bone. Try to create variety in the things you choose. A small piece of driftwood or a bone that has been sun-bleached can be used. A feather here and there adds interest.

By adjusting the length of each strand you can design the hanging just the way you want it until you change your mind. Then it can be rearranged again.

Secure a leather thong across the top of the disc. It should be hung so that it is fairly stable.

Other materials that you might use for the base of this mobile include: a piece of driftwood, a cross section of a tree that is sanded and varnished, or a disk of glazed pottery with holes.

Shell and Macramé Neckpiece

Macramé has been popular for so long that I am ashamed to admit that I have never learned to make anything using this crafting technique. Not only haven't I ever made anything, but I can't even make a knot. Nonetheless, there are so many exquisite projects being created that I wanted to include a design suggestion for using macramé combined with natural materials. It was time to call on an expert. My friend Elen Schwartz lives in Barbados. She spends a good deal of time doing macramé and creates projects for an island magazine. The nice thing about

A macramé, shell, and feather neckpiece by Elen Schwartz.

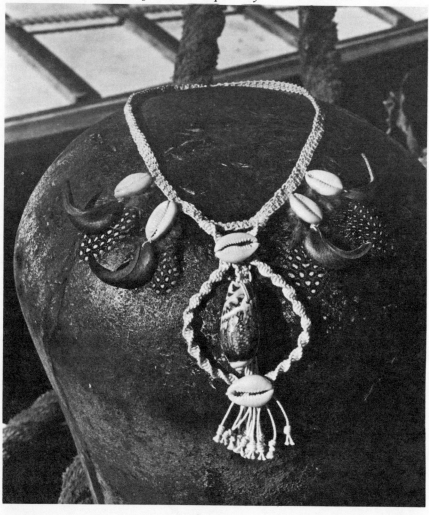

her work, which varies from a key chain to an elaborate plant hanger, is the delicate knotting and twine that she uses. Her projects are done with thin cotton twine that is sold in marine-supply stores. Could she please design a simple project with feathers and shells to share with us? I asked. Well it started out simply. After all, how much simpler could you get than six pieces of twine. But as she went along she became more and more carried away with the project, and I was completely lost. So for all of you who know how to do this craft I'm sure that Elen's design ideas will be an inspiration. If you don't know how, any beginning macramé book will have instructions for a basic chain, which you can then decorate.

Elen began by putting a cord around her neck to determine the desired length for the neckpiece. Measure three times this original length and double that before cutting. Divide and cut

Begin the macramé neckpiece with 6 pieces of twine, each approximately 36 inches long.

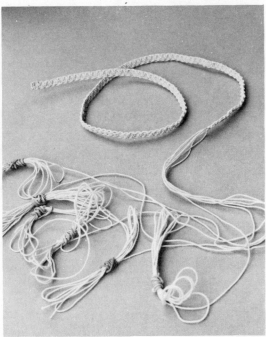

the pieces into three equal lengths. Find the center of each and place a pin at this point securing the strings to a board. There will be three lengths of string to work with on either side of the pin. Using a simple square knot, make a chain for the main part of the neckpiece. The centerpiece is a spiral knot, and the ends are joined together with a shell that is secured in the back with a square knot. So much for the macramé, and now you know why I have never done it.

The decorative elements are evenly spaced and secured along the length. Small holes will need to be drilled in the shells to attach them to the chain. Use a Dremel Moto-Tool, available in craft shops. First tie the shell and curved coconut shells together. The coconut piece has a tiny hole in the top. This curved shell comes from the coconut and is available from craft and shell shops. Attach this to the neckpiece by threading and tying it securely. The feathers are then glued onto the back of the shell and the end part is tied to the macramé. The tassels at

The shells and feathers are held in place with straight pins to determine the final design.

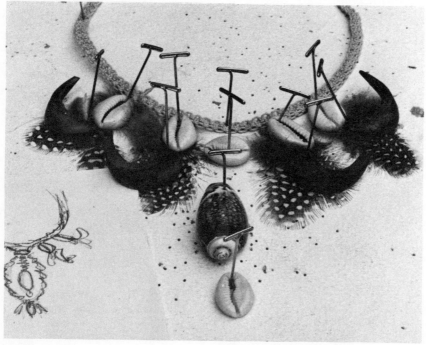

the bottom are cut from the excess string to the desired length
and have a coil knot at the bottom. A catch is added to the back
of the neckpiece. The overall design has an African feeling although made with materials easily available everywhere. The
shells were all purchased in a shell shop even though I am sure
Elen has used many of the shells available on the island beaches.

Detail of macramé neckpiece by Elen Schwartz.

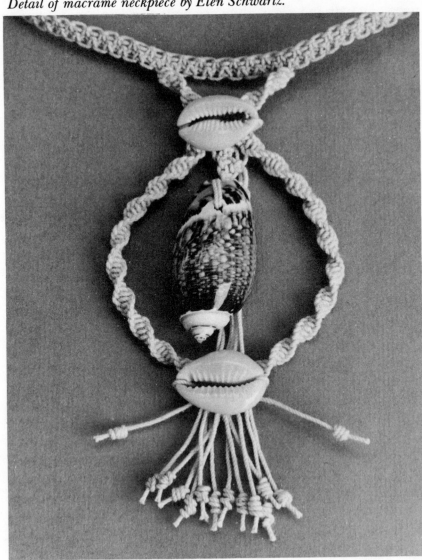

Shellcraft Techniques

In Victorian days shellcrafts were very popular. The ladies created shell flower arrangements, shell pictures, and collages. Sailor's valentines were also a popular shell art. Most shell projects involve gluing and arranging of the shells, and because of the many pieces involved it's best to be organized. This is particularly true if you will be working on many projects at once. A plastic sewing box or compartmented fishing-tackle box is excellent for holding everything in easy-to-find fashion. You will need quick-drying, clear-gluing cement. Shellcraft or 3M Super Strength is recommended. Tweezers and toothpicks are used to manipulate the shells. Cotton is used to form a bond between the shells and background. If you are making floral arrangements, you will also need green-covered floral wire, and a wide variety of shells that have been found or purchased.

Shell Flowers

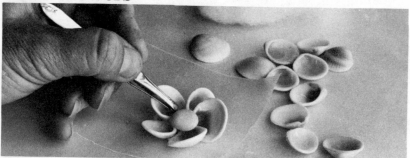

Almost all flowers can be recreated in shells. Lucine cup shells are good for this. Begin by placing a piece of plastic wrap or a plastic bag from the cleaners on your work surface. Place a dab of glue on the plastic. Saturate a tiny piece of cotton with glue and place it on the glue spot. Arrange the shell petals on the cotton by picking up each one with the tweezers and gently placing it on the cotton. Press the shells onto the cotton in a flower arrangement and allow to dry. The shell flowers are now ready to be adhered to any surface. If you are making a shell flower picture, be sure to have enough similar shells to create the arrangement that you want. Seaweed, secured in position with white glue, is good for stems and leaves. They can also be drawn in with a fine-tipped pen.

Sailor's Valentine

Sailor's Valentine by Charles McGuire

Sailor's valentines were popular in the early nineteenth century when whalers and trading vessels stopped in Barbados for supplies or to deliver cargo. There the seamen would purchase these lovely gifts made by the islanders to take back to their women. Some reports indicate the sailors also collected shells from the beaches so that they could make these valentines on the long voyage home. Perhaps the story was told in order to further romanticize the idea of the seafaring voyage. It is a pretty picture to imagine the sailors sitting on board, in the middle of the ocean, making petaled flowers out of shells.

Unfortunately, evidence for the romantic view seems slight. They do make unusual gifts, however, and today there is a renewed interest in the crafting of these valentines.

The traditional sailor's valentine consists of a shell motif, some geometric, some using a floral design, set into octagonal wooden cases that are hinged in the middle. When open they reveal two decorated sides. Each is like a glass-covered shadow box. They are usually twelve to sixteen inches in width and height. While many of the old valentines had a sentimental saying worked into the design, a valentine that you make might be created around a small mirror such as the one shown in color made by Charles McGuire. Mr. McGuire selects the delicate pastel shells found on the Florida beaches. Many of his elegant valentine mirrors are sold in exclusive Palm Beach gift shops. His designs reflect a more contemporary approach to this traditional craft.

If you want to make your own sailor's valentine you will need a lot of shells. Delicate jingle shells or the small lucine cup shells used to create the petal flowers are good for this. You can either make all the flowers the same using the same shells or you might like to experiment with a variety of shells and flowers. Tiny whelk shells are good to fill in areas between the flower shells. The principle for making the shell flowers is the same as shown in the Shell Flower Technique section.

If you cannot find an octagonal frame for this project, you might consider making one. While the octagonal frame was always used for the old valentines, you can set this project into a standard box or round frame which is easier to find. Frame shops carry all sizes, but first try to find an old, unusual frame in an antique or second-hand shop. A small mirror is the focal point around which the design is created. Since no two valentines are alike you can have fun creating your own design. When you have laid the shells out the way you think they look best, begin to glue them in place. A piece of glass cut to size will protect the shell valentine. (color plate #29)

Shell Basket

Basket filled with unusual shells from The Collectibles Ltd.

Often the simplest idea is the nicest. If you have collected some unusual shells, you could display them in a small basket. Perhaps you will choose to make a basket from the fields. It will look nice wherever you place it. The natural colors of the shells combined with the basket are quite subtle. Fill the basket almost to the top with florist's clay or a chunk of styrofoam. These are both available at a garden or flower shop. The shells are glued to this with Shellcraft glue or 3M Super Strength. They are both clear. Pile the shells on top of one another so that it looks natural. Keep the larger shells on the bottom so that the arrangement dosen't look top heavy. Glue each shell to the one under and next to it so that all the shells are glued to one another. You can make any size arrangement depending on the size of your basket and the number of shells to display.

Sand-cast Candles

Materials needed:
Candle wax
Candle colors
Candlewick
Wax hardener
Bucket of sand
Pan for heating wax
Mold for shaping materials such as,
  small bowls, wooden spoons
Meat thermometer (optional)

Sand has interesting properties that have attracted artists and craftworkers for centuries. Sand is a particularly good casting medium. It can be used to cast plaster and is excellent for casting large sculptural candles. The basic rules of sand casting are: 1. Keep it simple. 2. Think in reverse. 3. Don't stick your fingers in hot wax.

Make an impression in sand using a bowl or other household object.

Sand is not a precise medium to work with so it is best to keep the project simple. As for thinking in reverse, many people get confused when creating a hollow or negative cavity into which to pour something. You have to think of the empty space as solid.

The sand you use should be fine, not coarse such as that used in a child's sandbox. Aside from beaches, sand is available at lumberyards and building-supply companies. If you get it at the beach, sift the shells and debris out of it by pouring it through a screen.

The bucket or container holding the sand should be big enough to accommodate the size candle you want to make. You could use a box, but whatever you use be sure that there will be plenty of sand around all sides of the candle.

Directions: The sand should be wet—damp, but not dripping. It is fun to see how much variety you can put into the form of the candle. The basic design can be created by making an impression of a bowl or pot or ordinary can into the sand. This

Use small objects to make depressions in the sand.

Pour hot candle wax into the sand mold.

When the wax cools, loosen the sand around the candle.

will form the body of the candle. This is your mold. A solid base can be made by pressing a smaller can farther into the bottom of the mold.

Melt the candle wax in a coffee can that is set in a pan of boiling water. Wax can be very dangerous when hot, so be sure to set the can in water and do not leave it unattended. If there is not enough water to boil easily around the wax-filled can, the sputtering wax could start a five, should it directly hit the heat of the burners. Always supervise children in this sort of project. You will need three pounds of wax, which is purchased in a craft shop. To this melted wax add two tablespoons of stearic acid, which is the hardener and also available at craft stores. Stir in color if desired. This is a small cube of colored wax available in craft stores. You might want to add a candle scent, which is available right in your cupboard. Vanilla, nutmeg, or cinnamon can all be used. Simply mix in a teaspoon of your choice.

When the wax begins to cool off (if using a thermometer, the

Gently lift the candle out of the sand.

wax should be 150°) pour it into the sand mold carefully.

Finishing: When the candle is cool and hard, gently push the sand aside so you can get your hands under the candle. Remember that the sand is heavy and the wax is delicate, so do this gently. When the candle is removed, it will be covered with sand. You can leave it this way or you can brush it off carefully. The candle will not be completely smooth, however. If you like the sand-coated effect, you can make it more permanent by coating it with a mixture of equal parts of white glue and water.

With a hot wire feed the candle wick into the center of the candle.

To insert the wick, heat a stiff piece of wire such as a coat hanger, until it is hot enough to penetrate the candle to within an inch of the bottom. Use wire to feed wick into the hole.

There are many variations you can try once you know how to make the basic sand-cast candle. Look around the house for shapes to create the impressions you want. Handles, small boxes, small cylindrical bottles, sticks, fingers, bowls, and glasses can be used to make designs. You can even add legs onto the candle bottom.

Memory Pockets by Kathy Kelm.

Memory Pockets

In the hands of an artist, found materials can be a springboard for creative ideas. Kathy Kelm is an artist, persistent experimenter, and professor of textile design at the Rhode Island School of Design. However, her talent is expressed in various media including natural assemblages. Perhaps a memory box can be defined as the visual expression of a feeling that the artist wants to capture. The symbols are personal, yet we are free to enjoy them and read our own meaning into the box. Kathy describes her creation as a combination interrelation of tactile, visual, and emotional memories.

It is hard to look at Kathy's memory pockets without immediately wanting to do one. Each of us has little treasures hidden in a drawer or on a shelf that might create a meaningful statement when combined in such an assemblage. You might begin yours by using a theme such as love, freedom, beauty, nature. Perhaps memories of childhood or of a place that had special significance might be remembered with bits and pieces placed in memory pockets. A memory pocket can be a valentine, a wedding gift, or a reminder of some shared fun.

All you need are little ascetate boxes. These are the thin flexible ones that candy might come in. The frame is made to fit the exact number of boxes being used. Kathy has mounted the unit of boxes on a weathered-wood background that is decorated with feathers and fabric pompoms.

Kathy's memory box includes shells, coral, a drawing, a print, bones, feathers, a butterfly, and seaweed. The combination creates a fascinating assortment of textures, colors, values, and shapes. What does it represent? Only Kathy knows for sure.

Driftwood Hanging

Driftwood, like sea glass and stones, floats in from the sea. It has been treated and sanded by the sand and waves and the sun has bleached it to a silvery gray. It is usually smooth and soft in texture and all the rough edges have been sanded so that they are rounded and polished. Sometimes pieces of wood from a boat have been discarded to rot on the beach. These often have turned into interesting shapes. Even nail holes become more prominent exaggerating the defects so that they are no longer ugly. Collect what you can find. Perhaps you have access to a boatyard. This is a good place to poke around. Odd pieces of other found wood can also be used for a hanging decoration.

Our hanging is 5 feet long. If you can find enough interesting pieces to create a hanging this big, you should plan the design first on a piece of paper. Use brown wrapping paper and

Look for discarded pieces of wood for an assemblage.

A driftwood mobile.

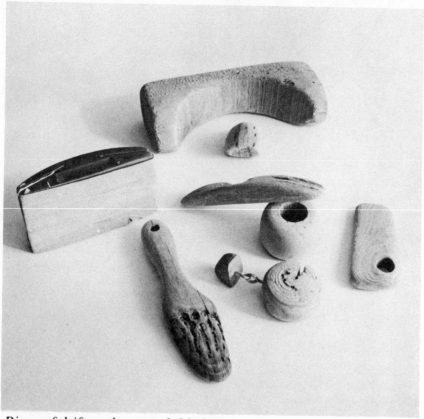

Pieces of driftwood are sanded before assembling into a mobile.

plan where you will place each of the pieces. If you don't have enough pieces to create such a large decoration, you can fill in with some that you make. Make a rough sketch filling in the shapes that are missing.

Making the missing pieces: A power sanding disk or a sanding disc that fits onto a power drill is the easiest method for rounding off wood to look beach worn. But it is quite easy even without power tools. Sometimes lumberyards have scrap piles that are treasure troves of wooden pieces of irregular shapes. All these need is filing with a wood file and a bit of sanding with coarse sandpaper.

Assemble your pieces and lay them out in the right order. The pieces are then attached with screw eyes. These come in many sizes. Use a large size such as ½": They can be part of the design and they will keep the wooden pieces just the right distance from one another. They are also easy to manipulate. Depending on the placement of the screw eyes, you can create all kinds of angles. Screw the eyes into all the pieces of wood. Then using a long-nose pliers, open one screw eye up just enough to join the two eyes. Close it up with the pliers and do the same with each successive piece until complete. Be sure to place one at the top for hanging.

Driftwood Wreath

Wreaths have traditionally been made of flowers, herbs, even vegetables. A most unusual and really beautiful design can be achieved using driftwood, bones, and shells. The silver and white almost aparkle. The design is very sophisticated and might be a new use for the sea treasures you have saved.

The backing for this wreath is made of Foamcore. This is a stiff cardboardlike substance that is found in art-supply stores. It is white in color and can be used as is. Begin by cutting out a circle for the wreath. To do this tie a 14-inch string to a push pin. Place the pin on the Foamcore. Tie the other end to a pencil. Stretch the string out and draw a circle with the pencil. Shorten the string to 10 inches and draw an inner circle. Cut the two circles out with a craft knife such as an X-Acto.

To this begin gluing the driftwood and bone pieces around the circle using white glue such as Elmer's. Place the material onto the circle as well as on top of one another to create an over-all pattern. Fill in with small shells. This wreath holds long narrow pieces that are similar in size and shape, which gives it the symmetrical-looking design. If you have shells that are the same size, this might be a different way for you to use them.

Bone Assemblage

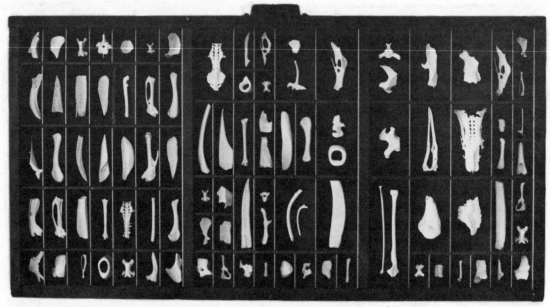

White bones and shells arranged in a type drawer for display by Ann Jones.

Johann Gutenberg had no way of knowing the service he was doing for craft people when he came up with the idea of setting type by hand. The movable pieces of type had to be stored in something, so it had to have twenty-six compartments for letters plus others for numbers. The type case that holds the type is an interesting artifact in that it has different-size compartments depending on the frequency of use of each of the twenty-six letters in the alphabet.

Using type cases to display collections of various sorts is not a new idea. Artists, craftspeople, and designers have been onto this idea for some time. But frequency of use does not diminish the creative potential of this idea.

The bone assemblages by Ann Jones are elegant examples. Ann has created compositions of exquisite proportion and sub-

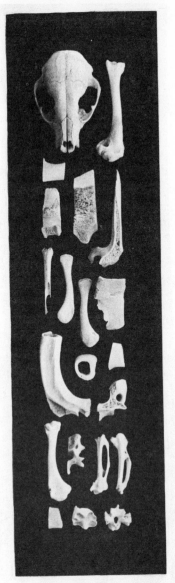

assemblage by Ann Jones.

tlety by the disciplined placement of the right form in the right compartment. Nothing is placed arbitrarily. It is not accidental art. It is just the opposite since the limitations are so stringent. There are just so many different bones that one may have on hand, and the compartments are of unchanging dimension.

Ann first painted the type drawer black. All the bones were found on the beach. While the sun bleaches bone to an almost uniform white color, Ann chose to paint them pure white to achieve a stark contrast of black and white in her composition. The bones are glued into position with white glue. The assemblage is then covered with a piece of ⅛-inch Plexiglas. This preserves the work from dust and adds a finishing touch.

Where to find type drawers: Type drawers are easier to find in and around large cities. Frequently antique shops have them. Auction firms and typesetters and printers are other possibilities. They should be more available as time goes on since many typesetters are switching from traditional handset type to phototypesetting and getting rid of the old equipment. If you are handy, you might make a display case that is similar in size and shape. Craft shops carry collectors' boxes which are crudely made, but can be used as display cases.

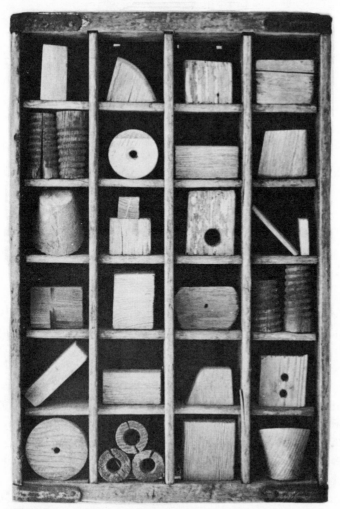

Wood assemblage 18" high by Ann Jones.

Wood assemblage by Ann Jones.

Nuts and pits found on the beach. Assemblage by Ann Jones.

Mail order sources for supplies

Basket making supplies:

American Handicrafts Co.
P.O. Box 2911
Fort Worth, Texas 76101

Cane and Basket Supply Co.
1283 S. Cochran Ave.
Loss Angeles, Calif. 90019

J.C. Larson Co.
7330 N. Clark St.
Chicago, Ill. 60626

Sax Arts and Crafts
207 N. Milwaukee St.
Milwaukee, Wis. 53202

Candlemaking supplies:

American Handicrafts
P.O. Box 2911
Fort Worth, Texas 76101

Barker Enterprises, Inc.
15106 10th Ave. S.W.
Seattle, Wash. 98166

Pourette Manufacturing Co.
6910 Roosevelt Way
N.E. Seattle, Wash. 98115

Corn husks:

Nitch in Time
1 North Riverside Rd.
Riverside, Ill. 60546

Decoupage supplies:

American Handicrafts Co.
P.O. Box 2911
Fort Worth, Texas 76101

Connoisseur Studio, Inc.
Box 7187
Louisville, Ky. 40207

Hazel Pearson
4128 Temple City Boulevard
Rosemead, Calif. 91770

The O-P Craft Co.
425 Warren St.
Sandusky, Ohio 44870

Flower arranging materials:

Boycan's Craft Supplies
Mail Order Division
P.O. Box 897
Sharon, Penn. 16146

Floral Art
P.O. Box 394, Highland Station
Springfield, Mass. 01109

Fran's Basket House
89 W. Main St.
Rockaway, N.J. 07866

Miss Plum's Particulars
66 Church La.
Westport, Conn. 06880

Herbs and spices:

Caswell-Massey Co. Ltd.
518 Lexington Ave.
New York, N.Y. 10017

Miss Plum's Particulars
66 Church La.
Westport, Conn. 06880

Wide World of Herbs Ltd.
11 Catherine St. East
Montreal, 129 P. Quebec Canada

Leather, beads and feathers:

Craft Yarns of Rhode Island, Inc.
603 Mineral Spring Ave.
Pawtucket, R.I. 02862

Freed Co.
Box 394
Albuquerque, N.M. 87103

Hollywood Fancy Feather
512 S. Broadway
Los Angeles, Calif. 90013

Lamb's End
165 W. 9 Mile Rd.
Ferndale, Mich. 48220

Naturalcraft
2199 Bancroft Way
Berkeley, Calif. 94704

Progress Feather Co.
657 W. Lake St.
Chicago, Ill. 60606

Tandycrafts Inc.
3 Tandy Center
Fort Worth, Texas 76102

The Southern Leather Co.
950 Perdido St.
New Orleans, La. 70112

Macrame supplies:

American Handicrafts Co.
P.O. Box 2911
Fort Worth, Texas 76101

Craft Kaleidoscope
6551 Ferguson St.
Broad Ripple Village
Indianapolis, Ind. 46220

Creative Handweavers
P.O. Box 26480
Los Angeles, Calif. 90026

P.C. Herwig Co., Inc.
Rt. 2, Box 140
Milaca, Minn. 56353

Macrame Weaving and
Supply Co.
63 E. Adams #403
Chicago, Ill. 60603

Seashells:

A.D. Starr & Son
190 South King St.
Suite 1956-A
Honolulu, Hawaii 96813

Florida Supply House Inc.
P.O. Box 847
Bradenton, Fla. 33506

Gooleni
11 Riverside Dr.
Suite 5 VE
New York, N.Y. 10023

Lamb's End
165 W. 9 Mile Rd.
Ferndale, Mich. 48220

Naturecraft
2199 Bancroft Way
Berkeley, Calif. 94704

Stained glass materials:

Boycan's Craft Supplies
Mail Order Division
P.O. Box 897
Sharon, Penn. 16146

Nervo Distributors
650 University Ave.
Berkeley, Calif. 94710

Whittemore-Durgin Glass Co.
Box 2065
Hanover, Mass. 02339

Weaving supplies:

Carmel Valley Weavers
1342 Camino Del Mar
Del Mar, Calif. 92014

Colonial Woolen Mills, Inc.
6501 Barberton Ave.
Cleveland, Ohio 44102

Craftool Company
1421 W. 240th St.
Harbor City, Calif. 90710

El Mercado Importing Co.
9002 8th Ave. N.E.
Seattle, Wash. 98115

Freed Co.
Box 394
Albuquerque, N.M. 87103

School Products Co. Inc.
1202 Broadway:
New York, N.Y. 10001